The New Deal and
American Politics

The New Deal and American Politics

A Study in Political Change

JOHN M. ALLSWANG
California State University
Los Angeles, California

JOHN WILEY & SONS
New York
Santa Barbara
Chichester
Brisbane
Toronto

Cover designed and executed by Mark E. Safran
Production supervised by Joseph P. Cannizzaro

Library of Congress Cataloging in Publication Data

Allswang, John M.
    The New Deal and American politics.

    (Critical episodes in American politics)
    Bibliography: p. 139
    Includes index.
    1. United States—Politics and government—1933—
1945. 2. Voting—United States. I. Title.
II. Series.

JK261.A64   320.9'73'0917   78-5733
ISBN 0-471-02515-1
ISBN 0-471-02516-X pbk.

Printed in the United States of America

10 9 8 7 6 5 4 3 2

FOR EDEN AND YAEL

Foreword

The resurgence of political history is one of the most interesting developments in recent American historical scholarship. In the years immediately following World War II, scholars tended to dismiss the study of past politics as mundane and old-fashioned as they focused on cultural, psychological, ethnic, and intellectual approaches to the American experience. But the enduring importance of political events, brought home to scholars as well as journalists by the tumultuous events of the 1960s and the devastating Watergate scandal, led historians to examine the political past anew. Many borrowed ideas and techniques from social scientists to probe into such new areas as voting behavior, party fluctuations, and the role of ethnocultural factors in politics. Others relied on more traditional studies of campaign rhetoric and the impact of charismatic leaders on the political process. The result was a new flowering of political history.

Critical Episodes in American Politics is a series of interpretive volumes designed to bring the new scholarship to bear on eight major episodes ranging from the origins of the first party system in the 1790s through the trauma of Vietnam and Watergate. Each author examines the political process at a critical time in the American past to demonstrate the way the democratic system functioned under great stress. Employing different techniques and approaches, each author seeks to explain the distinctive events in the period examined to give the reader an insight into both the strengths and weaknesses of the American political tradition.

In this volume, Professor John M. Allswang analyzes the impact of the New Deal on American politics, stressing the lasting consequences of the political coalition forged during the presidency of Franklin D. Roosevelt. The author combines evidence from a data base that includes the election results from every American county of the 1930s with more traditional historical sources to offer a perceptive—and sometimes surprising—interpretation of the New Deal coalition. Not only does Allswang examine the familiar national developments of the 1930s, but in addition, he studies the relationship between the New

Deal and both city and state governments. He notes the growing importance of the urban-federal connection and he describes the varying impact of Roosevelt's national policies on the individual states. The result is a new synthesis that provides a portrait in depth of the vital changes in the American party system, changes that influenced American politics through the 1960s, and in some ways still affect political behavior today.

Robert A. Divine

Preface

No other topic of modern American history has elicited so much general and scholarly interest as the New Deal. This is not really surprising, since the conjunction of the Great Depression, Franklin Roosevelt, and the New Deal comprised a period of unparalleled privation and hope, defeat and confidence. Moreover, it saw the most active government ever practiced in America up to that time, making our interest quite logical. There was a new sense abroad in the 1930s, common and even old hat nowadays, that government could deal with the economic and other problems that had grown with industrial America. This makes it a rather ebullient period, especially in the person of the presidential leader himself, and despite the very real and dismal sufferings of so much of the population.

Not least of the areas of American life influenced by the decade of the New Deal was politics. There were many important changes. Democrats replaced Republicans. National government replaced local and state. Activism replaced diffidence. A positive view of politics and government replaced a rather sceptical one. Groups traditionally weak in terms of political power suddenly found themselves key elements in the strength of a winner; and the traditionally most powerful elements of American society found themselves in the unusual position of regarding political affairs from the outside.

These political changes of the New Deal years were particularly important because they were hardly fleeting. It is nearly a half-century since Franklin D. Roosevelt was first elected president—an awesome enough thought for those of us who remember him as "our president"—and it is obvious that the effects of the New Deal were real and are still with us. This is true in many areas of American life, and especially so in politics. Our political life continues to focus on many of the same problems, and to work on many of the same bases and divisions, as were first introduced in the 1930s.

This book is a survey and an interpretation of the ways in which American politics was affected by the Depression, the New Deal, and Franklin D. Roosevelt. It is not a history of the New Deal, or of politics per se. Rather, it tries to show the effect of history on a variety of aspects of politics. Politics is defined here, quite broadly, to include popular political behavior and commitment, partisan strength and weakness, political organization from national to local levels, the relationships of various branches and levels of government, and more. Only with such a broad definition, I think, can we ever really gauge the effects of any major forces on our political life.

The book is highly indebted to the published and unpublished work of other scholars, who have probed in depth so many specific aspects of the decade. I have been less concerned with trying to generate new information about the New Deal than with essaying explanations and interpretation of important questions that seem to me to have been so far either unasked or unanswered.

What will strike some readers as the "newest" aspect of the book, I suppose, is the quantitative material I have used throughout. The data does comprise something new—albeit not the only new thing to be found here—because, of the hundreds of New Deal scholars before me, none has really tried to do a quantitative study of the New Deal on an integrated national–state–local basis. This is not surprising, since the data is very difficult to work with and not entirely satisfactory. I have had to compromise with data aggregated by counties, of which there were over 3000—providing sufficient work for myself and my computer. But counties are rather large units, in which specific economic, social, and ethnic groups and interests are not easily isolated. Thus, I have complete sympathy for my colleagues who have settled for individual city or state studies, or highly generalized national ones, where they could feel somewhat more comfortable with their data.

But pragmatists step in where the more rigorous fear to tread. It seems to me that suggestive data, as opposed to conclusive data, is better than nothing at all, and that this is absolutely true when it permits some understanding of historical problems for which conclusive data is just not available. Moreover, it is the interrelationship of the quantitative data and the other information here, rather than solely the one or the other, that gives the interpretation strength.

I have tried to keep the book's argument clear, even for those who have little knowledge of the period. This has required some background explanation. And I have kept the statistics simple, primarily percentages; there are coefficients of correlation, because they are useful. In the Appendix, I have described the data, the statistics, and the methods employed. Many readers might benefit from reading the Appendix first. All the numbers are here to provide information or analysis—not to confuse or make the book arcane.

In addition to the many scholars to whose work I am obligated, a debt insufficiently implied in the Bibliography, there are some people who have been especially supportive of my efforts. Eric Austin and Jerome M. Clubb of the Inter-University Consortium for Political and Social Research were very helpful in providing me with data and also in the beginning stage of analysis. Glen Dollar of the California State University and Colleges State University Data Center, and Richard McChesney of my own campus computer center were very cooperative when things went wrong through errors that were not infrequently my own. My good friend and colleague Bruce M. Stave of the University of Connecticut was typically enthusiastic and helpful. And Robert A. Divine of the University of Texas offered important suggestions and corrections. Ms. Marge Gilbert once again did a good job of manuscript typing. And Wayne Anderson, Rosemary Wellner, and Joseph Cannizzaro of John Wiley & Sons were all very helpful. None of these people, of course, bear any responsibility for what follows, which for good or ill consists of my own interpretations.

The data utilized in this book was made available by the Inter-University Consortium for Political and Social Research. Neither the original source or collectors of the data, nor the Consortium bear any responsibility for the analyses or interpretations presented here.

I am grateful to the Netherlands America Commission for Educational Exchange, and its director Ms. Joanna Wind, for financial support in the final stages of completion of this book.

My wife, Suzanne, as always, has been very supportive of my work, and for that I thank her. My children, on the other hand, have been neither very interested in it, impressed by it, nor helpful to me in getting it done; and for that demonstration of good sense I lovingly dedicate the book to them.

Leiden, Nederland   John M. Allswang
February, 1978

Contents

The New Deal and
American Politics

Prelude to the New Deal

Before one can begin to look at the effect of the New Deal on various aspects of American politics in the 1930s, it is important to understand some of the forces in operation immediately preceding the coming of Roosevelt. Especially important are the general political context of the United States in the 1920s, the nature and effects of the Great Depression starting in 1930, the political response of the Hoover administration to the Depression, and, finally, the campaign of 1932.

The decade of the 1920s was one of the high points of a long period of Republican domination of American politics. Starting with the Civil War, and accelerating in the mid-1890s, the Republicans established a hold on national politics so well-engrained that they remained the dominant party even in those years when the presidency, and even Congress, were in the hands of Democrats. Between the election of Lincoln and that of 1932, the Republicans won 14 of 19 presidential elections, controlled the Senate 62 out of 72 years, and the House 46 out of 72 years. From 1861-1875, again from 1897-1911, and once again from 1921-1931, they held control of both houses of Congress and the presidency. This was one of the longest such tenures in American history (to be exceeded only by the Democrats via the process studied in this book).

At the state and local levels there was, to be sure, more variety. The Democrats were firmly entrenched in the deep southern states, and often did well in parts of the northeast also. But our contemporary acquantance with the Democratic party as the "party of the cities" should not lead us to believe that this was the case prior to the New Deal. We shall see that the Democrats were on the rise in the urban centers, but they certainly did not have general urban strength: if New York City was run by Tammany Democrats, Philadelphia was controlled by Vare machine Republicans; if Boston seemed consigned to the Democracy, Chicago was often the opposite.

Most importantly, the Republicans were the majority party, and overall this crossed national-state-local lines. Their hold on the majority of the voters was well demonstrated in the decade preceding the New Deal, a decade labeled by at least one historian as "the Republican Era."

Beneath this strength, however, there were weaknesses, albeit often unseen in the 1920s. The Republican coalition was one essentially created in the 1890s. Through its innate strength, and the Democrat's factionalism and weakness, this coalition had maintained itself for over a generation. But a generation is a long time, expecially one like circa 1895–circa 1925, wherein the United States saw a tremendous increase in industrialization, urbanization, immigration, and modernization generally. The country in the 1920s was a very different place from what it had been in the 1890s, and with the wisdom of hindsight we can see that the Republicans had not really responded to those changes, that in fact much of their strength in the latter decade was based on a good deal of inertia, as well as the weaknesses of the Wilson administration and the Democrats.

So long as the real prosperity of the 1920s continued for most Americans, the Republicans appeared secure in their control of national politics. Whether or not this was only appearance is arguable but not provable, since the prosperity did come to an end; my own feeling, however, is that there were noneconomic forces in operation in that decade that presaged an end to Republican ascendancy regardless of the Depression. It has been well argued that major questions in American life are less often fought out between the two major parties than they are within the one party currently in power. This has certainly been true most of the time since the 1930s. But in the 1920s the Democrats were agonizing over the major new problems of American life, while the Republicans weren't really debating them at all.

Republican leaders of the 1920s, like Herbert Hoover who spoke contentedly of the "New Day" that had come to America, felt they had developed a formula for social and economic success, and the obligation of government was primarily to support the essentially private forces that had built that system. Other group and individual problems and conflicts were secondary, and would work themselves out in the new general prosperity that was filtering down to the entire population. They were optimistic materialists, sure that material well-being would resolve other kinds of tensions.

But they were wrong on several counts. First, even before the Depression, the tremendous economic growth of the United States in the 1920s almost entirely skipped some groups, like miners and most farmers. Beyond that, while the real wages of most workers rose, the distribution of the wealth created remained very much askew. Moreover, the country was confronted with a number of social and cultural problems every bit as important as economics, and which the Republicans were content to ignore.

About twenty-four million immigrants came into the United States between 1880 and 1920, bringing with them cultures, values, and aspirations of great moment to the country's future. Overwhelmingly, they shared the American preoccupation with security and material advance, but they did so from a distinctive frame of reference. They poured into the cities where the jobs created by industrialization were to be found, becoming at one and the same time (along with the rural Americans also coming to the same places at the same time and for the same reasons) the basis of the American proletariat and of urban America. The 1920 census was the first one wherein the urban population outnumbered the nonurban, and that was very important. Far more people worked for others now than for themselves, often in large factories where the worker's skills were minimal and could be learned in a matter of hours, or minutes. And such people lived as they worked—amidst bigness and insecurity.

The United States in the 1920s was a much more class-based and class-divided society than it had been a generation earlier. It was also culturally much more heterogeneous, and suspicious. Moreover, the major interests of both new and older Americans did not always follow the essentially economic paths that many politicians assumed. The rise of the Ku Klux Klan to national importance in the early 1920s suggested

3

the extent to which old stock Americans worried about the sociocultural directions America was taking—modernism in religion, decline of old values, cultural pluralism, and so on. Essentially law-abiding people were quite willing to go outside the law to maintain what, to them, had made America great.

Prohibition was even more important; for almost a century, starting about the time of Andrew Jackson, it was the consistently most tenacious and divisive domestic issue in American politics. Its passage as a constitutional amendment at the end of the Great War was a classic case of the success of a committed and organized minority. But its support was as much on cultural grounds as moral ones—it was, to its proponents, another way of establishing the hegemony of traditional American values, and traditional Americans, over new values and new people. And to the immigrants, Prohibition was not simply the denial of their right to drink, it was something willfully and maliciously foisted on them by old stock Americans.

In Chicago, for example, there were four opinion referenda on Prohibition between 1919 and 1930. Chicagoans voted on this issue between 73 and 83 percent anti-Prohibition. Newer, south and east European groups voted 88 percent anti; Germans voted over 90 percent anti, as did others. And this was in no way untypical of urban voting on Prohibition nationally in these years.

These sociocultural problems, however briefly described here, were very important, because they were central to politics. Many Americans demonstrated time and again at the polls that such matters as Prohibition, immigration restriction, and the Klan were at least as important— if not more so—than purely economic questions. And the economic questions they were concerned with often focused on power—union recognition—as much as immediate material return. The great weakness of the "progressive movement" of the early twentieth century was in its almost total disregard of such concerns; it had thus failed to attract the urban masses.

And the same can be said of the national Republican party in the 1920s. If it was the party of prosperity, it was also the party of immigration restriction, and of Prohibition; there was little dispute over these matters within the party during this decade. In short, the Republicans were, perhaps unknowingly, giving up by default the most rapidly growing segment of the population—and one, in terms of electoral votes for president, that was even more powerful than its numbers might suggest.

Partly, the Republicans ignored these problems because they seemed to be doing as well among these groups as the Democrats. But the Democratic party was undergoing change in the 1920s—painfully, slowly, but nonetheless substantially. This was in part for reasons of simple logic and the desire to win elections; but it was also due to a new generation of urban Democratic leaders who both empathized with and represented the new urban population groups, and realized that they comprised the Democrat's best chance of national success.

The bitterly divisive Democratic convention of 1924 is instructive. The acrimonious battles, and narrow vote divisions, over the nomination contest between William Gibbs McAdoo and Alfred E. Smith, and the showdown on whether or not to specifically condemn the Ku Klux Klan, demonstrated that issues of urbanism and ethnic heterogeneity were under debate among the Democrats. True, the urban and rural elements of the party fought to a draw in 1924, but at least the former was a contestant there. And in 1928, with the nomination of Smith, the urban element was dominant.

Indeed, the 1928 campaign, with urban, Wet, Catholic, Tammany-ite Governor Smith for the Democrats, against Herbert Hoover (a classic American Protestant success story) for the Republicans, pinpoints many of these forces very clearly, and anticipates much of the conflict we shall see in the 1930s. Hoover won, and quite strongly, largely on the basis of prosperity and traditional Republican sources of strength, plus some anti-Catholic Democratic votes, especially in the south. But, as scholars began to recognize quite some time ago, beneath the gross statistics one can see in Smith's support an important shift in the sources of Democratic voting—a shift, which, if it maintained itself, would be very important for the Democrats.

Table 1.1 gives a more specific demonstration of this change for one city: Chicago. And while not all cities responded as Chicago did, this was not an isolated phenomenon.

There is much debate among historians as to when and how the shift of urban voters to the Democrats began. Was it Smith or was it Roosevelt? Was it one critical election or a series of them? The answers to these questions are not central to my concern here, although I am convinced that it was a series of elections, and of candidates and issues, that built the "Roosevelt coalition" that is a central subject of this book. The important point is that, in national politics, there were strong indications before the onset of the Depression that the Republicans were in trouble and the Democrats were on the rise.

TABLE 1.1

Presidential Voting in Chicago for Selected Groups, 1920–1932 (Percent Democratic)[a]

	1920	1924	1928	1932
Czechoslovakians	43	40	73	83
Poles	39	35	71	80
Lithuanians	53	48	77	84
Yugoslavs	22	20	54	67
Italians	31	31	63	64
Germans	18	14	58	69
Jews	15	19	60	77

[a]Source: John M. Allswang, *A House for All Peoples: Ethnic Politics in Chicago, 1890–1936,* 42.

Moreover, while it is a bit more difficult to summarize, this does seem to hold for state and local politics as well. More and more local Democracies were realizing the political advantages—made so clear by men like Tammany leader Charles F. Murphy in New York—of a coalition of the poor and the new. In Boston, New York, Jersey City, Chicago, and smaller cities as well, the Democrats had begun to establish themselves in city halls—and state houses—on the basis of a new kind of politics. Success is its own greatest vindicator in politics. Franklin D. Roosevelt and his advisers could not plead a lack of guidelines when he made his race for the presidency.

Having argued that the Republicans were weaker than their electoral victories in the 1920s indicated, we must now turn to a brief look at the Great Depression of 1930–1940 as another force of tremendous political importance in the coming of the New Deal.

It is very difficult to communicate the gravity of the Depression to those who are removed from it by a generation or more. It was not only the economic loss involved, but the psychological and spiritual effect of privation accompanied by lack of hope that hurt so many people so badly. Conversely, Roosevelt's and the New Deal's offer of hope, even if couched in rather unclear proposals, would have an opposite effect.

The economic crisis deepened rapidly after the stock market crash in the fall of 1929. Dollars not spent have the same kind of multiplier effect, negatively, as dollars spent tend to have. Thus, each job lost, or payroll cut, or materials or equipment request cancelled, ramified and magnified in its effect on the economy. When the depression hit its nadir, in the winter of 1932–1933, about one-fourth of the labor force was out of work, approximately thirteen million people. The number of partly unemployed and underemployed was equally great, to say nothing of the previously unemployed (young people especially) who were unable to enter the work force. As early as 1930, in an ordinary small city like Ann Arbor, Michigan, retailers, real estate firms and other businesses, not getting their usual income, began to find themselves unable to pay their own bills. From there it could only spread.

For the unskilled and semiskilled, there was usually nothing to fall back on. Only one-half of American families had savings accounts in 1930, with an average balance of only $339 (for whites; for blacks it was only $150); this was not much of a cushion—and when the banks started failing in large numbers in 1932, it could even mean that money was unavailable. So the urban working class was in an often untenable position. Jobs were the key, and they were increasingly unavailable; relief, as we shall see, was totally inadequate. Not surprisingly, many tried, and others considered, radicalisms of one kind or another.

For middle class people the economic effects were real, though sometimes less crucial. Nonetheless, many lost their jobs entirely, others found themselves descending to inferior economic and social status, which was, to them, a terrible blow. Perhaps their sense of loss was simply greater because they had lost more. One student of the Depression in farm areas concluded just that—that various kinds of farm protest were greatest in areas of high land values and relative farm prosperity, and lowest in the most traditionally depressed farm areas. This generalization certainly would apply in the early Depression years to the south, where the sharecroppers, the poorest of the poor—black and white alike—did little, for there seemed to them little that one could do.

There was a great deal of hunger in America in the early 1930s; there was also some starvation, and a lot more deaths due to diseases that would not have led to death had people been better nourished. There were hundreds of thousands of people, especially the young, on the roads, roaming around for want of anything to do, and in search of their next meal. There were scores of thousands without lodging, camped in parks and vacant lots in all the major cities. There were, in short, dozens of reasons for millions of people to be depressed in spirit and bereft of hope. And Americans did respond to the promise of success, or at least the surface attractiveness of various kinds of imported and domestic solutions for the ills of the nation.

What made it all so much worse was that the United States, true to its optimistic and capitalistic traditions, was unprepared for the emergency, and to a good degree unwilling to respond with the kind of aid that, it was argued, would help people in the short run only to harm the nation eventually. The welfare and relief systems of the United States were still essentially preindustrial: they were locally organized, using either private philanthropic funds or modest state appropriations. This was a system that had never been really good, and in the Depression it witnessed what one historian has called "the breakdown of local resources." It was unlikely such a system could work in 1930; and, given the traditional suspicion rural state legislators had of the cities anyway, plus the insistence of business groups that the crisis would only disappear if it were ignored, disaster was inevitable.

Philadelphia, for example, had one of the nation's highest unemployment percentages in 1930; it also had a tradition of private philanthropy. In November 1930 a private commission was formed, the Committee for Unemployment Relief, to administer city funds. It was well run, and received from the city the three million dollars that the latter had been authorized by the state to borrow. But this sum was never enough, which became truer as the months went by. If the committee was able to spread its first million dollars over a whole year, a later five million went in three months. In the spring of 1932 there was a period of eleven days when the Committee had no dollars at all. Those who received money got too little; others who needed it got none. This experience led even one banker to look toward that traditional enemy of the people, government action: "The present need is on a scale that calls not for more charity but for governmental action to save the health and indeed the lives of a large portion of the citizenry."

There was nothing distinctive about Philadelphia in this regard. By 1932 especially, most cities were like Philadelphia in percentage of unemployed, degree of want, and inability to respond. Smaller cities and towns were often worse off, since their economic base was narrower and more precarious. What was most obvious and most grueling about the Depression was not the gross statistics of lowered production, investment, and output, but rather the blatant human suffering, misery, and degradation that was taking place all over the country. More people were in greater and more basic need in America in the early 1930s than at any time in memory.

Business leaders, blindly confident in the system that had built industrial America, insisted that the crisis had to be endured; it would rectify itself. Writers and preachers, echoing the sentiment, urged people to find ways to make money—sell things, be creative, work for whatever one could earn; it was up to the people to prove their mettle, and to defeat the Depression. Local and state politicians, lacking answers and sharing many of these niggardly values, said the same thing, or else argued that the problem was national and thus beyond them. Ordinary people, urban workers and farmers alike, whose lack of education perhaps stood them in good stead vis-à-vis economic theory, realized that these conservative arguments—sincere or not—were nonsense. And they turned, with more and more other groups in the population, to the national government.

Since the days of Theodore Roosevelt this trend at least had been clear: in an America increasingly national in its economy, society, and intellectual outlook, the role of the national government must inevitably increase. This idea was always controversial; it seemed sometimes most acceptable to a president, sometimes to Congress, occasionally to the federal courts—but the idea survived deep and constant criticism. The 1920s was perhaps its lowest point, but the Depression reestablished it, and by 1930 and 1931 all kinds of people looked to Washington, and especially to Herbert Clark Hoover.

Hoover failed, and failed abysmally. He failed to solve the economic crisis or even to halt the economy's downward spiral; he failed to halt the human suffering that was a basic part of that crisis; he failed to give inspiration to a dispirited populace; he failed to provide, in Washington, the leadership the disparate elements in American society had come increasingly, even desperately to hope would be found there. And he failed, quite obviously, to make any political gain for himself or his party in this process. It did not require solving all these problems to develop some real popular support in America; it did at least require an image of caring, and trying. Hoover managed neither; and he failed at reelection. Roosevelt, in doing not much better with the basic problems of the Depression, but a great deal better with the easing of immediate human suffering and with providing an image of leadership, was reelected three times.

Hoover, like most of us, was a captive of his own experience. If ever a man, in terms of material wealth, power, even of philanthropy, was an ideal example of the correctness of traditional American values, it was he. Born and reared in abject poverty, he had made himself into a college graduate, a young millionaire as a mining engineer, a superb administrator in food relief during the Great War, an outstanding cabinet member under Harding and Coolidge. He had been an ideal, if nonpolitical, choice for president as a capstone to the Republican 1920s. And he was entirely convinced of the validity of traditional American values and the wrongness of tampering with them.

In some ways Hoover the businessman was among the most ideological of American presidents; individualism, localism, private enterprise, property rights—these were the things that had made America great and Americans prosperous. And he firmly believed—as a truly ideological conservative—that, however unhappy the evils of the Depression might be, the Depression was a short-term phenomenon that would be overcome by traditional means. Conversely, any meddling with the system, any national government activity that interfered with individualism and localism and private enterprise and property, would be a disaster; it would undermine not only the economy, but also human freedom and democratic institutions. The true misfortune, for Hoover and the American people, was that he largely lived up to his beliefs, and was powerful enough as president to keep the activities of national government consonant with them.

It is true, as has been frequently pointed out, that Hoover was not entirely insensitive to the need for federal action to deal with the problems of the Depression, especially after the election of 1930 when he had a marginally Democratic and increasingly liberal Congress pushing and poking him. He also developed some sense of the necessity for at least the image of action if he really wanted to get reelected in 1932. We need not here catalog the legislation passed and nearly passed, which Hoover sometimes supported and sometimes vetoed. Suffice it to say that, despite some willingness to experiment, he remained true to his traditional economic and moral values: the federal government should balance its budget; it had neither economic, constitutional, nor intellectual reason to interfere with local prerogatives or private concerns. Thus, the monies appropriated by the federal government were small relative to the crisis, and Hoover-thinking administrators spent them slowly even after appropriation. Moreover, more of that money went to the support of private businesses than to hungry individuals— this was because of Hoover and Republican economic theory, perhaps, more than from class loyalty, but in terms of political effect the reason did not matter.

Others, looking at the mixed results of the New Deal's tremendous spending programs, can debate what, from a policy standpoint, Hoover ought to have done. But from a political standpoint it is obvious that he failed terribly. It was Hoover and his party whom the jobless and hungry blamed. More and more, especially in the hurtful year of 1932, he came to personify for many Americans the evils and the injustices associated with the Depression.

Perhaps nothing demonstrated his tenacity and his political insouciance better than his reaction to the famous Bonus March of 1932. Here were 20,000 to 25,000 bona fide veterans of the Great War, out of work through no fault of their own, and asking only for payment now, rather than in 1945, of the service bonus that Congress had already agreed to pay them. When the Congress refused to legislate what they wanted, some left, but most members of the now-named Bonus Expeditionary Force stayed on for want of anything better to do. They were law-abiding and cooperated with the police while they camped on in Anacostia Flats across the Potomac.

Hoover, as often, was more reasonable than many of his advisers. He was willing to support legislation to pay their way home. But beyond that he would not go, and with the passage of time he came to agree with his political, business, and military advisers that it was a dangerous situation (General Douglas A. MacArthur was convinced that they were "animated by the essence of revolution"). After some violence took place in removing veterans from the Treasury Building, Hoover sent in the army, under MacArthur ("We are going to break the back of the BEF"), with Eisenhower and Patton also in attendance—it was admirably led. The rout was efficiently carried out, not brutal; but nonetheless two veterans were shot to death, more were injured, and thousands were in effect treated as outlaws.

It was a sad spectacle, in some ways an epitome of the insensitivity of the Hoover administration and its supporters to the human problems of the Depression. It got the kind of press it deserved. And it took place in July of a presidential election year, when the incumbent really hoped for reelection; it can hardly be classed among the wiser political decisions in the history of the American presidency.

Finally, we come to the national elections of 1932, which put Franklin D. Roosevelt into the White House and the New Deal into American life. We have already seen the major reasons for the electoral result; here we shall look briefly but directly at the election and some of its characteristics.

Among the Democrats, the real battle had been in primaries and the national nominating convention, to see who would have the good fortune to run against the Republicans in this very opportune year for an opposition party. The Democrats' rebound in the 1930 mid-term elections, combined with the steady economic decline since then, gave the party real hope.*

Roosevelt had been a leading Democratic vote-getter in the New York gubernatorial races of 1928 and 1930. Thus, he had been among the potential candidates for some time. We need not expand on Roosevelt's campaign for the nomination here. He had been working hard, with an extremely efficient organization—directed by James A. Farley and Louis McHenry Howe—since 1928, to the point where only Al Smith posed a real threat if the nomination was decided in the early balloting. He was seen in the party as a conciliating force, having good relations with all regions and groups, with no strong issue stands or personal characteristics that offended any important party elements; in short, he was highly "available," if not necessarily very exciting.

The Democrats in the convention and campaign tended to minimize issues, letting the Republicans try to defend a very sorry case. The Democratic platform was very short, the Republican one very long. But there was not much the latter could say that the public would believe. The Depression was a gruesome reality. And some of the other issues of the 1920s still festered, working to the Democrats' advantage. This was especially true or Prohibition. When the philosopher John Dewey complained that "We are in the midst of the greatest crisis since the Civil War and the only thing the two national parties seem to want to debate is booze," he demonstrated only his own ignorance of the sociocultural depth of that issue, and the fact that to the voters it was a very real issue even in 1932. The Democratic platform and candidate were clearly wet, the Republicans dry. And it was one more force for a Democratic victory.

Roosevelt carried 57 percent of the popular vote, and 42 of the states. Large Democratic majorities were elected for the House (312–

---

*Actually, the 1930 congressional vote was fairly distinct from later New Deal voting. If we look at correlation coefficients, nationally 1930 related to the 1932 presidential vote at .741; regionally, it was .477 in the urban northeast, .654 in the south, .162 in the middle west, and .546 in the mountain states. These are fairly low intervote relationships. Party meant less in 1930, and switching was still underway at the congressional level. We will see stronger relationships between subsequent elections. See the Appendix for description of statistics, data, and methods.

TABLE 1.2

Selected Correlates of 1932 Presidential and Congressional Voting by Region, for Counties[a]

Region	Presidential Vote	Congressional Vote
NORTHEAST (over 250,000 pop.)		
Pop./square mile	.535	.561
Foreign stock	.460	.353
Old stock	−.480	−.385
Black	−.161	−.053
Urban	.484	.468
Unemployed, 1930	.303	.251
SOUTH (under 250,000 pop.)		
Black	.386	.274
Farms owned	−.595	−.609
Farms tenanted	.622	.622
MIDWEST (under 250,000 pop.)		
Foreign stock	.330	−.578
Old stock	−.395	.517

[a]Pearson's r. See Appendix for description of statistics, data, and methods.

123) and Senate (59–37). Democratic strength was general, and national: very strong in the south, at or above the national average almost everywhere except in parts of the northeast, especially New England. Table 1.2 provides more detail. In the northeast, Roosevelt built on and extended Al Smith's 1928 strength among urban groups, workers, and immigrants and their children. In the overwhelmingly Democratic south, he was particularly strong among the poor tenant farmers. In the nonurban midwest, none of the correlates are very striking.

On the whole, support for Roosevelt and for Democratic congressional candidates was essentially the same. The new president did somewhat better among the foreign stock in the big cities, and considerably better in the nonurban middle west. But on the whole it was a party victory. Indeed, one study of presidential and congressional voting from 1920 to 1964 found the election of 1932 the second lowest (after 1936) of all in terms of the amount of split-ticket voting. This suggests the extent to which the election victories of the 1930s were Democratic partisan victories, and also the effect of Roosevelt as a party unifier. He both contributed to, and benefited from, the great Democratic party strength that began to appear in 1932.

TWO

☆

Forces for Political Change

In examining the politics of the 1930s, it is necessary to look directly at Franklin D. Roosevelt, and at the New Deal, to see what they did and how they operated to directly or indirectly influence political development. In ensuing chapters I view this from the standpoint of the acted-upon—probing the perceptions and reactions of various groups of Americans. In this chapter, however, the focus is on the actors in Washington, and what exactly they did or seemed to do, and felt or seemed to feel, which was of political importance.

The New Deal—its legislative and other programs, its personnel and their motivations—has been analyzed and debated extensively from its inception. It has been described and divided on a chronological basis ("First" and "Second" New Deals), an ideological one ("cooperative" and "swing to the left"), a political one (nonpartisan followed by partisan), even a priority one ("relief, recovery, reform"). Each analysis has been countered by its opposite, or varieties thereof. All this is not surprising since the policies and programs of the New Deal were so numerous and various, and because Roosevelt himself was resistant to ready classification. So many groups and individuals were affected by

New Deal programs, and in different ways, that there was as much contemporary confusion as there has been retrospectively.

One reason for the difficulty in rationalizing the New Deal into any one convenient category is that Roosevelt himself was only intermittently an ideologue. He was also far from profound as an economic thinker. He moved back and forth as the exigencies, human or political, required. His motives varied, from human need to economic theory to political reality, with many stops in between. Moreover, especially in the early years, the initiatives for what became most striking in New Deal programs came neither from Roosevelt nor from his advisers, but from Congress, where insistence on employment programs, for example, was most strong.

The famous Hundred Days, the very productive first three months of the Roosevelt presidency, were a good example of the variety of approaches the New Deal would take, of the internal dynamics of the federal government, and of the ways in which Americans would be influenced by the New Deal. The frenetic pace was often more impressive, and influential, than the legislation itself. And this was nowhere more true than for the emergency banking bill presented to the special session of Congress called for March 9, 1933. The bill, which was quite conservative and essentially a Hoover administration measure, was read to the House to save time, and became law the same day.

Passage of legislation to amend the Volstead Act to permit wine and beer was almost as swift, as was action to begin the process of repealing the Prohibition Amendment. The first Agricultural Adjustment Act reflected a conservative response to the consensus among farmers on what they needed, especially price supports; it was by no means especially geared to the small farmers, or the tenants who we have seen to have been such great Democratic voters in 1932. Congress added to the farm bill an unrequested grant to the president of powers to apply inflationary pressure on the nation's money; and the president used that power to take the country off the gold standard. It was also congressional initiative that produced the first large ($500,000,000) appropriation for relief, in direct grants to the states.

Roosevelt was leery of public works proposals that might not prove to be really worthwhile, but he was even more opposed to the dole. The Civilian Conservation Corps seemed a workable approach, and he and Congress agreed on it rapidly. He did also accept a $3.3 billion public works appropriation that was attached to the National Industrial Recovery Act, and, unlike Hoover administrators, most New Deal managers were not reluctant to spend what had been appropriated to them.

The Home Owner's Loan Act was certainly not anti-business, since it guaranteed the mortgagor as well as the mortgagee, but it saved many homeowners from losing their homes to foreclosure. The Farm Credit Act did the same for farmers. Fully twenty percent of American homes and farms were ultimately refinanced through the agencies set up by these statutes.

The establishment of the Tennessee Valley Authority, on the other hand, was more controversial. The idea of long-term and comprehensive government planning, as well as that of government "competition" with private enterprise, did not sit well with more conservative Americans. But this first regional planning for the United States did provide hydroelectric power to an area badly in need of it, as well as fertilizer production, flood protection, land conservation, and recreation. It was one of the most ambitious of New Deal programs.

The National Industrial Recovery Act was probably the best expression of Roosevelt's own moderate and cautious approach to the problem of recovery. He realized that in the country at large, and in Congress as an expression of the nation, there were real and conflicting interests. And he wanted, for reasons of belief as well as expediency, to side with none of them. So the NIRA was a compromise, giving to business exemption from the anti-trust laws so firms could cooperate to overcome industrial stagnation, and giving to labor in the famous Section 7(A) a guaranteed right for collective bargaining. There was also, to reassure those who insisted on planning and federal government supervision, a government licensing provision. And, as we have seen, a large public works appropriation was also added to the legislation.

There were many reasons to see the Hundred Days as neutral, as not necessarily so anti-business as many had feared. On the other hand, business interests disliked any fiscal "irresponsibility," or even very much federal interference. They felt 7(A) was such an interference, and many were unhappy with the Securities Act, which gave to the Federal Trade Commission considerable power over the securities business, and made directors of corporations civilly and criminally liable for misrepresentation. The Glass Steagall Act, separating commercial from investment banking, also had direct effect on business enterprises; and the amendment thereto, establishing the Federal Deposit Insurance Corporation (which Roosevelt at first opposed), saved hundreds of banks from following the path of total failure so common in 1932, as well as providing to the average depositor a security never before possessed.

In sum, the Hundred Days was a period of rapid, even frantic government activism, unprecedented in the amount and effect of its legislative program. That program itself was a combination of conservative and radical, of class-directed and general, of congressional and executive initiative. It was as noteworthy in its grants of traditionally legislative prerogatives to the executive branch as anything else. It demonstrated to the American people that the national government was concerned with their problems and willing to act; whether those actions would be effective, or were even proper, and who would benefit most from them, were questions not yet answered in June 1933.

After this first rush, the legislative pace slowed down a bit. Among other things, a good deal of time and effort was required to develop the administrative machinery for relief (the Public Works Administration under Secretary of the Interior Harold Ickes and the Federal Emergency Relief Administration under Harry Hopkins), the agricultural legislation, and, especially, the National Recovery Administration.

In the face of the coming of the winter of 1933–1934, with still vast numbers of unemployed, the Civil Works Administration was created, to administer relief directly rather than through the states. This was a first, and it was successful for its short life, doing a tremendous amount of building across the country, along with other activities, and carrying large numbers of Americans through the winter.

In 1934 came the passage of the Securities Exchange Act, which established the Securities Exchange Commission, with considerable powers to oversee the securities industry. The Communications Act established the Federal Communications Commission, to oversee radio and telegraph. And the Railroad Retirement Act provided for pensions for workers in this traditionally federally regulated industry. So far as New Deal leaders were concerned, the orientation of the administration continued to be neutral in terms of class and economic interests. But more and more business people disagreed, as we shall see; they were reacting both to the substance of New Deal legislation, and to the generally increased power and activism of the federal government. More and more, also, they found the New Dealers personally disagreeable and somewhat threatening. Labor leaders, on the other hand, and other representatives of the masses, were increasingly supportive.

These concerns became greater during the "Second Hundred Days"

of 1935. This rapid flow of legislation was itself at least partly motiva-
ted by New Deal leaders realizing the need to move leftwards in order
to stay in tune with most American voters. Roosevelt was himself often
trailing along behind the more radical measures, being persuaded ultimately by congressional and administration leaders that it was the path
of political necessity if nothing else.

The Social Security Act of 1935 was in many respects a very conservative piece of legislation. The only purely federal aspect was old age
pensions, and by financing these with a special payroll tax rather than
general revenues the administration was being fiscally regressive. Similarly, to operate the unemployment, indigent, and dependent aid
aspects through a federal–state arrangement was also clumsy at best,
very likely to result in much variation from state to state, and be hard
to manage. Both these compromises were perhaps necessary, given political realities and traditional American values. Moreover, however
imperfect, the creation of the Social Security system was epochal in
American history—a real, if diffident, commitment on the part of national government to the guarantee of certain minimal standards of
living for all citizens regardless of their situation.

The National Labor Relations (Wagner) Act was less wishy-washy.
It was a clearly pro-labor piece of legislation, and extremely important. It placed the power of law and the national government behind
the right of workers to organize, and of the majority of workers to
choose a bargaining agent for all; and it outlined and banned a list of
unfair labor practices, to be supervised by the new National Labor
Relations Board. The New Deal thus inaugurated the greatest period of
union growth in American history, and facilitated the organization for
the first time in large numbers of the unskilled factory workers of the
country. Perhaps no piece of New Deal legislation was as clearly class-
oriented, or as effective in changing the lives of so many people, and
the nature of the American economy, as this one statute.

The new "wealth tax" and the law strictly regulating public utili-
ties holding companies were also less "neutral" than earlier New Deal
legislation. The creation of the Rural Electrification Administration
meant that the 90 percent of American farmers who lacked the things
associated with electric power could now have them. And the Banking
Act of 1935 did what the one of 1933 had not: it established much
greater centralization and control of the American banking system, and
of the Federal Reserve, and significantly augmented the government's
role therein.

Finally, the general period of the Second Hundred Days also saw a considerable increase in the relief effort. Although Roosevelt still wanted the government out of relief, the continuing human need of twenty percent unemployment forced him to go against his instincts. Already, in January 1935, the Emergency Relief Act had appropriated five billion dollars, the largest single appropriation in American history to that time, for work relief. The money was spent by several agencies, the most famous ultimately being Harry Hopkins' Works Progress Administration, which hired people as laborers, builders, teachers, artists, chroniclers, and for myriad other purposes. The WPA tried to do what the country needed, whether it be building bridges or raking leaves or translating foreign language newspapers; in the process it was hiring people not only for jobs that supported their families, but also for jobs with which they were familiar. The aid was to be not only economic but also psychological, and benefit the public as well as the jobholder. The Public Works Administration under Ickes also built on a gigantic scale. And ancillary agencies like the National Youth Administration served more specific needs, in this case the giving of part-time employment to over two million high school and college students. However controversial, the federal relief effort did employ millions, and influenced more.

The second Roosevelt administration was much less ambitious legislatively, finding the administration of the laws already enacted quite enough to do. Perhaps the most important additional activity, in 1938, was the beginnings of anti-trust activism by the Justice Department, and, among the most controversial of New Deal laws, the passage of the Fair Labor Standards Act, which established the first federal minimum wage and maximum hour standards. The latter legislation affected only a small number of workers at its commencement; nonetheless it was another major step in increased federal regulation of the American economy and American business, and it was bitterly contested by economic and regional, especially southern, opponents.

One area of domestic concern was notable in its absence. The New Deal did not include any major civil rights legislation, nor any other direct attack on racial segregation in the south. The most important civil rights proposal of New Deal years was the bill to make lynching a federal crime. But even this modest proposal was unacceptable to Roosevelt and other New Deal leaders for fear of alienating the south. As Roosevelt put it to Walter White of the NAACP, "If I come out for the anti-lynching bill now, [the southerners] will block every bill I ask

Congress to pass to keep America from collapsing. I just can't take that risk." And while the New Deal was not inactive on the racial front, as we shall see, it was nonetheless unwilling to use legislation for this American problem as it had done for so many others.

It is quite impossible to separate the New Deal from its chief architect, Franklin D. Roosevelt. I want now to look directly at the president, "that man in the White House," to try to understand him a bit better, and to try to gauge the ways in which he personally was a force of significance in American politics during this time. In particular, I am seeking those personal characteristics, and actions, of the president that seem to me influential in the realm of politics.

Roosevelt had established himself as a "presence" of sorts early in his career, beginning his public service as a Democratic New York state legislator from a traditionally Republican district. Even in his losing effort to become vice-president in 1920, he had impressed those voters and politicians whose paths he had crossed. This impact was hardly diminished by his impressive and dramatic recovery from crippling poliomyelitis. And in his first gubernatorial campaign, in 1928, when he won in a Republican year, one student of his campaigning concluded that his ability to impress the voters personally had been the margin of his victory.

Roosevelt also had the advantage of being our first "nationally advertised" president, whose everyday personal and official life was detailed to the public. This was only partly due to the gravity of the Depression, or to FDR's own character; it was equally a function of the development of radio and other national media of communication and persuasion, of the rise of public opinion studies and reporting, and of a better educated and more interested public.

But such developments were a loaded gun, which could work for or against a given public figure depending on the person's abilities. And here Roosevelt was a master, as one student of his technique aptly summarized: ". . . the sound of his golden voice with its warmth and confidence; . . . the vision of that infectious smile as shown in the newsreels and candid shots . . . the magnificent presence of the man who appeared serenely before millions although he could not walk; . . . the visions of hope which his words aroused."

The president's famous "fireside chats," making very productive use of the relatively new medium of radio, are a good example of his skills at mass persuasion and influence. The first, explaining the emergency banking bill of March, 1933, was probably more important than the legislation itself in calming fears and persuading Americans that their banks were in fact safe. He used this technique repeatedly, establishing the appearance of a kind of president-to-citizen intimacy that had not existed previously. The image was of a man very sure of himself, a bit patrician, a bit authoritarian—but certainly a leader, and a caring one at that.

Roosevelt's speeches were also well done, and in some respects he might be said to have initiated the modern press conference. Wilson had been the first to hold meetings with the press, but, as one student has put it, the vehicle "reached its peak" under FDR; no one has exceeded him at it yet. Roosevelt's press conferences were useful in a number of ways; like his successors, he used them not only to reply to reporters' questions, but also to convey—via "background" and "off the record" items—additional information that he wanted disseminated without attribution. Thus the president simultaneously manipulated news reporters and also contributed to a much more open and knowledgeable presidential press. He used his press conferences to sway public opinion behind his person and his proposals, in his disputes with Congress or the courts for example. It was another tool available to the modern presidency; Roosevelt saw this, and took advantage of it. Like the fireside chats, the press conferences established his presence as the leader, and kept his avenues of approach to the masses quite direct. Had television existed in the years of the Roosevelt presidency, one wonders if he would have lost any domestic battles at all.

Another medium, often ignored, was the mail; for Roosevelt it was very important, both outgoing and incoming. He was always a good detail man, whether in terms of political or policy decision, or personal relations. He also learned from his two political mentors, Louis Howe and Jim Farley, the importance of personal contact and the usefulness therein of the mails. As early as 1928 Roosevelt was playing a national role, corresponding with Democratic politicians all over the country, making suggestions and asking for opinions. The pace of all this stepped up once the decision to push for the presidency had been made. Farley was a compulsive, but hardly careless, letter writer, who maintained a truly national correspondence with party workers and influentials, and impressed on Roosevelt the need to communicate and maintain relationships.

Into the White House this phenomenon continued, but at a rapidly expanding pace. The mail he received was so large that an entirely new system had to be devised to receive, categorize, and respond to it. Howe and Farley, and FDR himself, were highly aware of the political importance of this mail, and the danger of ignoring or otherwise ill-using it. A letter well-answered could produce many votes (thus when a Pennsylvania black wrote about the possibilities of moving black voters to the Democratic party, the letter was routed to Pennsylvania Democratic leader Joe Guffey for answer and action); a supportive letter could be very useful in press releases or press conferences; the quantity of letters could be used to move a recalcitrant Congress—all these things were understood and acted on.

Roosevelt continued throughout his presidency to be an active correspondent, keeping in touch with old friends, politicians, influential business and labor people, and many others. His wife was equally active, if not more so. And the professional letter writers in the White House mail room were under careful supervision to see that every letter was answered, and in the right way.

In all of these things Roosevelt demonstrated an implicit understanding of the way to success in a democratic political system. He saw that one needed to walk the line between demonstrating authority and seeming dictatorial, that one must be elevated but not remote, that one need not appear essentially "one of the people" so long as one appeared obviously for the people. He worked in the area of image as well as that of action, and in both cases was concerned with the mass of the people, and with important groups and leaders as well. Perhaps most important, he was able to draw a direct connection, in Americans' minds, between the New Deal and himself; they were one, and what was persuasive in one of them transfered to the other.

In more purely political aspects of action, Roosevelt once again was very shrewd. When necessary, he usually knew when to give in or to roll with the tide and often managed to turn it into something less than defeat. In the case of the Wagner Act, for example, he had almost openly opposed the bill when introduced, but once it had passed the Senate and seemed likely to pass in the House, he suddenly declared it "must legislation" and got a good deal of the credit for its passage. His relationship to massive public works appropriations was similar. Rather than fighting the inevitable, he was often able to turn it to his own advantage, and to get personal credit for what was actually congressional initiative. When he ignored what seemed inevitable, as in his Supreme Court battle, he could be seriously injured.

The foremost example, and politically most important by far, of

Roosevelt's ability to move in the right direction is the Second Hundred Days. The potential political power of new mass movements had reached threatening proportions by early 1935. Huey Long of Louisiana, Father Charles Coughlin of Michigan, and Dr. Francis Townsend of California were the most important of the new demagogues. But there were numerous other, smaller and more local movements that were also significant; the radical farmer groups had potential, and the near-success of Upton Sinclair's EPIC movement campaign for governor of California in 1934 was another indication.

Roosevelt and his advisers were highly conscious of the development of these organizations, and of the potential political ramifications if their tentative gropings toward amalgamation came to fruition in 1935 or 1936. Increasingly, it appeared that there was a direct conflict between Roosevelt's desire to keep the New Deal on a neutral, nondivisive track, on the one hand, and the kind of action necessary to undercut these mass movements on the other. Given the political stakes, and the number of voters involved, Roosevelt opted for the latter. Thus was born the Second Hundred Days, and Roosevelt's own continuing success at the expense of his rivals.

Roosevelt was an advocate of the carrot rather than the stick when possible. Better to persuade people with appointments, or appropriations for their states, or patronage power, than to have a direct confrontation. This was one of the reasons he was notoriously ineffectual about firing people—he preferred to alienate no one. It also explains part of the reason for his reluctance to take a more ideological stand for the New Deal before 1935. But when his back was against the wall, on things he considered important, he could be intransigent; in the Supreme Court battle, for example, he instructed Farley to hold up on judicial and other appointments in states whose senators were not supportive, and to use patronage to strengthen those who were more agreeable.

He was quite aware of the power of his office, and of his leadership of the Democratic party, and not averse to using that power when necessary, And as a corollary, he was aware of the importance of the state and local politicians who had the votes. If he sometimes seemed to people like Farley insufficiently partisan in some matters, he more often upset the ideologues of Congress and the media by his clearly partisan political actions. But FDR understood that, however disagreeable a Mayor Hague of Jersey City or any of a number of southern congressmen, these were the people on whom his successful coalition was built.

He was aware of the need for balance in other ways as well. By 1936 there was more and more gossip that he and the New Deal were too close to the Jews and the Catholics. His response was not righteous indignation, but rather the hiring of a former editor of the *Christian Herald* to join the campaign organization as its emissary to the Protestants; his assignment was to bring "Feminism, Piety and Pacifism" back to the Democratic camp.

Kindly dissimulation was also practiced, and with success. The best example came early in the first term, when the Bonus Marchers returned to Washington, with the same demands they had made of Hoover the previous summer. Roosevelt shared his predecessor's economic views and did not want to pay the bonus, but rather than the cavalry he sent 600 tents, along with latrines, showers, mess halls, and so on, and made sure the marchers got three meals a day. He offered employment to 25,000 veterans in the CCC (within a few weeks, 2600 did join). And he sent his wife out to see that they were well taken care of, and understood whence their good fortune came. It was a response both well-intentioned and politically sagacious, and helps explain the difference between the electoral success of the two presidents.

In sum, Roosevelt was one of the most impressive and charismatic of American presidents, a popularity exaggerated, to be sure, by the difficult times in which he operated. He was influential because he was able to move the mass of Americans (as late as 1949, in a poll on the greatest person living or dead, FDR received by far the highest number of votes), and command their support. He was skilled in politics as well as mass persuasion, and maintained leadership of an immensely popular political party. Combined with the legislative record of the New Deal and his own executive actions, Roosevelt's personality and personal leadership played prime roles in conditioning the nature of politics in the 1930s and after.

I have focused my discussion in this chapter on Roosevelt personally, and the New Deal institutionally, because they seem to me to be, in addition to the background factors discussed in the previous chapter, the key forces influencing the politics of the time. There were obviously some other forces at work during the period that also had an effect and are worthy of mention, even if briefly.

To a certain degree the New Dealers, as a distinct group of people, had an influence separate from the New Deal as an institution. The New Dealers and the leading New Deal politicians were to some degree separate: James Farley and Louis Howe were clearly among the latter, while Frances Perkins and Harry Hopkins represented the former. But, however much it might seem irregular, it was a good deal more likely for a New Dealer to get immersed in politics than the other way around. Partially this was because what they were trying to do was so innately political, and required persuading Congress, or placating a governor, or whatever. But also it was because many of the New Dealers were zealous in their socioeconomic goals, and even ambitious in their association with power. Thus, even so originally nonpolitical a figure as Aubrey Williams, administering the NYA and state relief administrations, became very much involved in the politics of relief.

Moreover, some of the New Dealers, like Harry Hopkins and Eleanor Roosevelt, very early were persuaded of the importance of politics—that everything was in fact political. Hopkins became enamored of it, and personally ambitious. Whether or not he really said that the Democrats would "spend and spend, tax and tax, and elect and elect," he certainly realized the interrelationship of these forces.

Eleanor Roosevelt was a national figure in her own right. In part, this was because she truly assisted her husband, and gave him an extended mobility that his lack of time and physical handicap denied him. But also involved were Mrs. Roosevelt's own ideological/social commitments and personal ambition. Her popularity rivaled (but did not match) that of her husband; she was certainly more ideological and idealistic, probably brighter as well. A generation later she would probably have sought and achieved major office for herself; but then she was a roving ambassador for the president, and an issue-oriented force within the New Deal itself.

If Roosevelt's administration acted in such a way as to provide aid of one kind or another to workers, blacks, the down-and-out generally, his wife was the one who made open personal commitments to their causes. Roosevelt felt he could not take the personal risk of offending the south by supporting an anti-lynching bill, or civil rights; but his wife could do this (as did Harold Ickes) without such political effect. Her commitment was sincere, but it was also of immense political value: the president placated one group, his wife placated that group's antithesis—and both voted Democratic, as we shall see.

In her travels, speeches, newspaper columns, and so on, Mrs. Roosevelt created a presence of her own, which was highly esteemed and very useful. Scholars differ on her motivation, the extent to which it was simple moral commitment, an effort to establish her own personality, or maybe just a desire to get away from her husband—but in a political sense her motives are irrelevant. She epitomizes the important individual, but never totally independent, role that New Dealers played in influencing the politics of the decade.

The more purely political people around Roosevelt—Howe, Farley, congressional and local party leaders—played a complementary role. His personal advisers had earlier helped Roosevelt, as we have seen, develop his personal style and effectiveness. And they continued to aid him after his election. It was Howe, for example, who insisted that every piece of White House mail, even when the rate was as much as 8000 per day, receive an individual reply, which alluded to the specifics of the letter and thus did appear truly personal and responsive.

Farley and some of the congressional party leaders played an important role, with Roosevelt, in seeking constantly to broaden the New Deal's voter coalition. Thus they looked toward nonDemocratic sources of support, and worked on alliances with groups like the Non-Partisan League and the Progressives in the upper middle west. They also played well the game of juggling various, sometimes conflicting interest groups to keep both traditional and new Democrats as happy as possible, and developed an unprecedentedly close relationship with party workers at all levels. Their success was most clear in 1936 when the entire Democratic party coasted to an overwhelming victory, with less split-ticket voting than in any other election between 1920 and 1964.

As noted above, the relationship between Roosevelt and the New Deal, on the one hand, and the Democratic party on the other, was obviously close and reciprocal. The success of the president affected that of his party, yet the opposite was also true. And as the party grew increasingly successful, on the state and local as well as national levels, it created its own internal dynamic, its own local reasons for maintaining its coalition of voters, that filtered up as well as down in creating success. If Roosevelt and the New Deal persuaded many people to vote for Mayor Kelly and his organization in Chicago, it was equally true that the Chicago machine persuaded many people to vote for Roosevelt and the national Democratic party.

27

Thus, causation exists on as many levels as response. And this goes well beyond the innately political. Successful New Deal legislation for collective bargaining created an increasingly powerful and wealthy independent agency and force for Democratic voting. Welfare did the same. The deeper our analysis goes, the more variables we find entering into the political equation.

But it was the Depression itself, the pre-New Deal political tradition, and Congress and Roosevelt in the New Deal that were the prime forces of political influence for the 1930s. Having briefly tried to sketch their development and nature, we can safely turn to the major focus of this book: the ways in which politics at various levels was influenced by the forces we have seen.

☆THREE

The New Deal and the People

The New Deal's most important political effects were those it had directly on the people. Political power in a democratic polity rests, ultimately, on the masses; and majority party strength rests on the coalition of voters and voter groups that that party can consider loyalists. Thus, in this chapter we look at the popular response, especially in terms of voting, that Americans made to Roosevelt and the New Deal, and the important and enduring political changes that resulted.

The consistent Democratic voting of so many groups of Americans in the 1930s, building on the forces already discussed, resulted in the famous "Roosevelt Coalition" that has largely dominated American national politics from 1932 to the present day. The coalition has been somewhat fluid, as such coalitions inevitably are over time, and there are signs of real ruptures in it since the 1960s; but its reality for thirty years is incontestable, and for the present certainly still arguable. Its origins are in the way American individuals and groups responded to the political forces of the time.

Roosevelt and the Democrats won handsomely in 1932. The new president won 57 percent of the popular vote and carried forty-two of

29

the forty-eight states, an electoral vote victory of 472 to 59. He carried every state south and west of Pennsylvania, and a total of 2721 counties (out of a national total of about 3100)—more than any Democrat had ever won before. The new House would be about 71 percent Democratic, and the Senate 62 percent. Twenty-seven of 33 gubernatorial races also went Democratic. The Democrats were in control.

In 1934 the Democrats added twelve more representatives and nine more senators to their congressional total, giving them over 70 percent of each house. Democrats also won twenty-three of thirty-two gubernatorial contests. And when Roosevelt ran again, in 1936, both houses of Congress further increased totals, to over 75 percent Democratic; and twenty-six of thirty-three state house races also went Democratic. Roosevelt triumphed personally as well, carrying all but two states, with over 60 percent of the popular vote and an electoral vote majority of 523 to eight.

The year 1938 saw the effects of the political and economic difficulties of Roosevelt's second administration. The Democrats lost 72 seats in the House and six in the Senate, as well as 17 of 31 gubernatorial races. This left them, however, with 60 percent control of the House and 72 percent control of the Senate, so it meant attrition from unprecedented power but hardly precipitate decline. The Democrat's success after 1938, at all levels, confirmed this assessment.

Table 3.1, which gives the correlation coefficients of each national election of the period with each other national election, shows that the bases of Democratic support remained pretty consistent. Both over time and across levels (presidential to congressional) the elections relate to one another at a very high level. And in 1938 the party's decline was general but not steep. This suggests that the Democrats' success was increasingly partisan in nature—a party, rather than personal or situational coalition, was being built. The table also suggests some difference between presidential and congressional coalitions, a condition that would be increasingly true in the ensuing generation.

It is difficult, because of the nature of my data, to find many very meaningful statistics that describe social or economic correlates of Democratic voting on a national basis (see Appendix). Therefore, in Table 3.2, I have put together some of the correlates of Democratic voting by region; the data is still county data, and thus more gross than one would like, but the regional subdivision does yield some insight that cannot be seen nationally. I will try to get yet more precise below by looking directly at some individual population groups.

TABLE 3.1

Correlations of National Voting, for Counties, 1930–1938 (Based on Percent Democratic)[a]

	1930 Congress	1932 President	1932 Congress	1934 Congress	1936 President	1936 Congress	1938 Congress
1930 Congress	—	.741	.867	.853	.706	.802	.861
1932 President		—	.832	.893	.906	.826	.882
1932 Congress			—	.892	.782	.826	.882
1934 Congress				—	.797	.878	.934
1936 President					—	.832	.780
1936 Congress						—	.893
1938 Congress							—

[a] Pearson's r. See Appendix for description of statistics, data, and methods.

TABLE 3.2

Correlates of Democratic Voting, by Region, for Counties, 1930–1938[a]

Urban Northeast

	Pop./Sq. Mile	Percent Old Stock	Percent Foreign Stock	Percent Age 18–20 in School	Percent Illiterate	Percent Urban	Percent Unemployed, 1937
1930 Congress	.379	−.187	.172	−.029	.036	.359	.059
1932 President	.535	−.480	.460	−.276	.268	.484	.464
1932 Congress	.561	−.385	.353	−.272	.227	.468	.360
1934 Congress	.423	−.251	.199	−.336	.184	.370	.166
1936 President	.344	−.180	.107	−.533	.215	.381	.412
1936 Congress	.510	−.194	.103	−.484	.169	.370	.309
1938 Congress	.310	−.198	.140	−.377	.210	.457	.249

Nonurban Farmbelt

	Percent Old Stock	Percent Foreign Stock	Percent Age 18–20 in School	Percent Rural–Farm	Percent Farms Owned	Percent Farms Tenanted
1930 Congress	.451	–.492	–.005	.071	–.020	.073
1932 President	–.395	.330	–.303	.279	–.108	.008
1932 Congress	.517	–.578	.006	–.071	–.083	.182
1934 Congress	.424	–.463	.107	–.178	–.224	.344
1936 President	–.324	.286	–.074	–.148	.014	–.024
1936 Congress	.462	–.498	.076	–.125	–.208	.244
1938 Congress	.533	–.566	–.036	–.121	–.012	.139

Nonurban Mountain

	Percent Old Stock	Percent Foreign Stock	Percent Age 18–20 in School	Percent Rural–Farm	Percent Farms Owned	Percent Farms Tenanted
1930 Congress	–.313	–.217	–.255	–.218	.115	–.092
1932 President	–.253	–.085	–.270	–.161	–.016	–.019
1932 Congress	–.181	–.264	–.228	–.263	.057	.018
1934 Congress	–.385	.272	.025	–.231	–.001	–.042
1936 President	–.456	.306	–.001	–.360	.037	–.124
1936 Congress	–.242	–.022	–.089	–.343	.120	–.111
1938 Congress	–.262	–.173	–.212	–.384	.253	–.180

Nonurban South

	Percent Old Stock	Percent Black	Percent Rural–Farm	Percent Farms Owned	Percent Farms Tenanted	Percent Farms Tenanted Noncash
1930 Congress	−.243	.303	.130	−.340	.347	.292
1932 President	−.375	.386	.269	−.595	.622	.558
1932 Congress	−.288	.274	.239	−.609	.622	.554
1934 Congress	−.322	.252	.034	−.412	.415	.346
1936 President	−.433	.471	.132	−.582	.598	.498
1936 Congress	−.343	.320	.059	−.556	.546	.441
1938 Congress	−.305	.239	.054	−.326	.320	.269

[a]Pearson's *r*. See Appendix for description of statistics, data, and methods.

In the more urban counties of the northeast we can see at least partial substantiation for generalizations about the role of the city and its people in the rise of the Democratic party. The positive correlations (at about as high a level as we will get with data aggregated by county) for population per square mile and percent urban indicate the general importance of city voting to the Democrats. The correlations for old stock are less negative, and those for foreign stock less positive, than one would expect, but this is again due to the nature of the data. Nonetheless, the decline in the level of correlation after 1932 is the reverse of what one should expect, whatever the general level: with the decline of general reaction to the Depression and concomitant development of firm party alliances for selected groups to the Democratic party, the correlation should have risen after 1932. I shall look at this problem again in the next section.

The role of the poor in the rising Democratic coaliton in the northeast is demonstrated in two other variables. The percentage of children age 18 to 20 who are still in school is a reasonable measure of wealth, and it correlates negatively with Democratic voting. Conversely, the positive correlation between percentage unemployed in 1937 with Democratic voting, especially in 1936, suggests the same thing—an inverse relationship between wealth and commitment to the Democrats.

Turning to the more rural areas of the midwest and the mountain states, there is a suggestion that the towns were more Democratic than the farms, especially in the mountain states—in the correlations with percent rural farm. Whether one owned one's farm or was a tenant, on the other hand, does not seem to have made a consistent difference in either area. And in both areas the figures for percentage of those 18 to 20 in school suggests that the poorer residents were somewhat more Democratic in the early years of the Depression, but that this difference disappeared by 1934.

The data on old stock and foreign stock differ somewhat for the two areas. The mountain states had relatively less significant relationships in this regard than the farmbelt, which did have a somewhat greater foreign born population. And in the farmbelt, the positive relationship was between old stock and Democratic voting rather than its opposite. This suggests that it was not the rural cousins of urban immigrants who comprised the Democratic resurgence in this area in the 1930s. But there are major exceptions in the two presidential years, where the relationships flipflop. The constituencies for congressional and presidential Democratic voting seem to have been somewhat different. (This can also be seen in farmbelt regional interelection correlations: the relationships between voting Democratic for Roosevelt in 1936 and voting Democratic for Congress in 1930, 1932, and 1934 were: $-.014$, $-.033$, and .138—far below the national figures we saw above.)

Finally, the south as a region is very hard to deal with simply because it was so overwhelmingly Democratic all the time. The most notable statistics are those related to rural wealth and its apparent effect on Democratic voting. The correlations for percentage of farms owned, and tenanted, with Democratic voting offer a strong suggestion that poorer southern farmers were even more allied to the Democratic coalition than their wealthier colleagues. Farm tenants did not differ much whether they tenanted for a cash rent or a noncash rent, but overall farm tenants were very strongly Democratic. Farm owners, on the other hand, seem the statistically largest part of the few defectors from Democratic voting. Logically, these differences were at their highest in the deep Depression year of 1932. And this, like some of the figures on the urban northeast, offers the suggestion that it was the gravity of the Depression more than the subsequent New Deal programs that precipitated the greatest reaction from poor Americans.

The slight positive relationship between percentage of the population that was black, and Democratic voting, probably does not signify that blacks were more Democratic than whites. Most of the black population, after all, was disfranchised. Rather, blacks tended to live in the areas of greatest rural poverty in the south—areas that we have seen were mostly Democratic anyway. And where the black population was greater, the percentage of whites (most of them old stock throughout the south) was lesser—which explains the modest negative correlation between being old stock and voting Democratic. It is important to put our statistics in context if they are to mean anything at all.

There are a couple of indicators, other than voting, that are also useful in demonstrating the general popular reaction to Roosevelt and the New Deal. One of these was the White House mail, which I have already discussed from the standpoint of the New Dealers' political activities. It is also worth mentioning as a measure of public support. The American people had been writing the White House at least since Lincoln; and in the pre-FDR twentieth century about 400 letters were received for the president each day. But in Roosevelt's first week he got 450,000 communications, and in late 1933 was still averaging 4000 to 8000 per day. The level dropped off a bit after 1933, but still remained far above pre-New Deal levels. Put in terms of daily number of letters per 10,000 population: Lincoln in the Civil War received 44, Wilson in World War I received 47, and FDR in 1933 received 160; even in 1938, Roosevelt's level was 111 per 10,000 Americans.

Thus, the quantity of correspondence between the citizenry and the president was unprecedented (it also rose markedly with other offices of the national government as well). Equally striking was its content. As usual, many letters were requests—for jobs, pardons, support of one kind or another; and the New Deal political leaders' careful responses to these letters were potent political weapons. But many also were highly personal, supporting or opposing policies or personnel sometimes, and other times simply expressing a need to communicate with Roosevelt. People confided in the president, asked his advice or prayers relative to very personal matters, and so on.

This is hardly something that can be measured in any precise way. But one can say that far more people, of all conditions of life, wrote expressing a personal involvement with Roosevelt than with any other president before him or since. This kind of empathy, as much as voting behavior, validates the famous remark of Will Rogers after the 1934 elections, when he mused on the Republicans' pre-election argument that "the Roosevelt honeymoon is over": "They were mighty poor judges of a lovesick couple. Why, he and the people have got a real love match and it looks like it would run for another six years." Even Rogers underestimated Roosevelt's appeal—by two elections.

Beyond writing letters, Americans also had a new way of expressing themselves starting about the same time as the New Deal: the public opinion polls. The mid-1930s saw the start of the first really reliable polls, especially those of Dr. George Gallup. This also marks the beginning of what over time will be one of the great repositories for the study of mass history in democratic polities.

The source of the 1936 New Deal Victory, for example, was anticipated in Gallup Polls on the issues in 1935 and 1936. Eighty-four percent of the public approved of old age pensions in late 1935, a measure of the extent to which Social Security had been successfully sold; and at the same time, 96 percent opposed the Townsend Plan, which was an even greater evidence of the relative success of the president on this issue. Strong public endorsements also emerged for continuing the CCC (82%) and for the success of labor unions (76%). So here was a basic source of support in the general public, industrial workers, and the unemployed.

New Deal farm policy did not fare as well, with only 41 percent approving. But the rise of federal power offended the traditionally localistic American public less than one would have thought: on the question of concentrating power in federal or state government, 56 percent opted for the federal government. Keynesian economics, however, was as illogical to the public as it was to Roosevelt himself, with 70 percent of the people in late 1935 feeling the budget should be balanced; about the same number also opposed currency inflation. The issues obviously were important to the public in terms of the way in which people were directly affected, and not in terms of ideological change.

Fortune magazine polls in 1936 found about 30 percent of the public viewing Roosevelt's reelection as essential, and another 30 percent as preferable to any alternative—this 60 percent total was almost exactly his share of the popular vote. Further breakdowns of the results tend to reinforce what we have already seen in our voting data: regionally, the south was most pro-FDR, at 81 percent, followed by the northeast (58%), the west (52%) and the midwest (49%). Younger people were more likely to favor the president than older ones; evangelical Protestants, Catholics, and Jews considerably more likely than members of the more middle class Protestant denominations. Finally, those classed as "prosperous" were only 42 percent pro-FDR, while those classed as "poor" supported him by 74 percent.

The reaction to Roosevelt personally, and especially his specific sources of support, changed very little to the end of decade, although the level of that support did vary somewhat. General reaction to his effort to pack the Supreme Court in 1937 was very negative (only 24% of Democrats supported him on this in late 1937, and 51% opposed him). But even at the New Deal's lowest ebb, in mid-1938, he still retained the support of 55 percent of the general population; this included 75 percent of the poor, 85 percent of the blacks (an indication of the striking change in that group's vote); 78 percent of factory and farm laborers, and 70 percent of the unemployed. The tendency of those still unemployed in 1938, or newly unemployed as the case may be, not to fault the president is noteworthy.

The polls are useful in filling in some data that my voting figures lack. They are also helpful in that they tend on the whole to reinforce what traditional sources and the data on voting have already suggested.

To really develop some sense of who, among the American people, became committed Democrats as a result of the Roosevelt presidency and the New Deal, it is necessary to switch our focus from geographic areas to population groups. And the American working class is as reasonable a group to start with as any other. Workers, particularly those in the cities, became a mainstay of the New Deal coalition, responding to the variety of ways in which the New Deal affected and improved their lives.

New Deal relief activities provided employment, and psychological relief, to millions of people—often only temporarily, but nonetheless significantly. Many other New Deal programs also had direct effect on workers lives, from protecting their bank deposits and mortgages to guaranteeing them against destitution through unemployment or old age or illness. The second New Deal, particularly, was class-oriented to a considerable degree—offering a cautious but real change in the orientation of government toward the working class masses.

This was even clearer in regard to trade union development. On the eve of the Depression, labor union membership had declined from a World War I high of over five million, to only 3.4 million; and at the depths of the Depression it declined even more, below the three million mark. Given the fact that most large-scale manufacturing industries had never been organized at all, this meant that the trade union movement was in very bad shape. But with the NIRA, and then especially the Wagner Act, the percentage of workers unionized in the United States jumped from nine to thirty-four. Regionally, in the east, midwest, and west, few citied avoided the tremendous organizing drives of the decade. The south, and the smaller cities and towns, experienced this less, which is one reason for their variant political behavior as well.

The change was not only one of government guarantees of the right to organize. Rather, through its legislation and through the beliefs of such pro-labor administrators as Frances Perkins and Harry Hopkins, the New Deal produced a government commitment to making unionism strong. Under the Wagner Act the government became the rule maker in and overseer of labor-management relations; the executive branch assertively executed the legislation passed by Congress. And it was this involvement that produced the great victories of the AFL and then the CIO in the big industries of the country.

The organizing drives had another effect. Not only did they quadruple the number of union members, and increase by tremendous numbers the businesses and communities that had to deal with union organization—they also served as vivid, sometimes violent witness to the degree to which the United States had become a nation of classes as a result of industrialization. It has been truly noted that the New Deal generally had the effect of clarifying, even exacerbating, class division in this country; in the process it also made clear to workers the usefulness of class, as a rallying-point, and as a rational way to understand their society and their own relationship to it.

Thus, as much as the changes in national government affected labor, so too did changes in labor's political policies ultimately affect national government. Quite logically, labor leaders in the 1930s forsook their traditional tactic of "rewarding friends" and "punishing enemies" without partisan associations, for a new one of firm partisan alliance. Labor's leaders, money, and votes were all part of this commitment.

The Democratic party had become, in the eyes of most workers, their party; and organized labor had become a key element in Democratic party affairs. Roosevelt played an important role in all of this, especially after 1935. He had his CIO man, Sidney Hillman, and his AFL man, Dan Tobin, to facilitate communication. He had overwhelming working class support, personally, and it spread to his party via legislation and hard campaigning. This bore its first obvious fruit in the creation of Labor's Non-Partisan League—which was not very nonpartisan—in 1936. It proved one of the foremost fund-raisers and vote-getters within the Democratic coalition.

This commitment on the part of labor can be seen only partially in voting data. In Table 3.3 I have considered the percentage of each county's labor force engaged in work in manufacturing industries. (Unfortunately, data on union members is not available.) The table shows the difference in terms of average Democratic vote, nationally and for the urban northeast alone, for the lowest (under 33%) and highest thirds of percentage of workers in manufacturing. The figures are consistent, if not overwhelming. The higher proportions of manufacturing workers were voting more Democratic. This was particularly true in the 1936 elections, when the effects of the second New Deal were more immediate; it diminished but did not disappear in 1938.

The American working class must also be defined in terms other than those of trade unionism. Indeed, it is the largely working class social and cultural groups that one often thinks of first in terms of the New Deal coalition: Catholics, Jews, the foreign born. And a strong appeal was made by New Deal politicians, who understood the reality and importance of the ethnic and religious, as well as economic, bases of American politics.

TABLE 3.3

Democratic Vote of Counties with High and Low Percentages of Workers in Manufacturing[a]

(Percent Democratic)

| | National | | Urban Northeast | |
	High	Low	High	Low
1930 Congress	69	58	48	43
1932 President	71	69	55	50
1932 Congress	59	64	55	49
1934 Congress	68	66	53	51
1936 President	77	66	62	57
1936 Congress	78	64	56	53
1938 Congress	68	63	50	45

[a]See Appendix for description of statistics, data, and methods.

With Catholics, for example, it took some real effort, despite the fact than many Catholics were traditionally Democrats and many more had been moved toward the Democracy by Al Smith in 1928. This, plus the effects of the Depression and the Democratic plank against Prohibition, seemed strong argument for continuing Catholic defections to the Democrats. But some Catholic groups, especially in the northeast, were unhappy about the scuttling of Al Smith in 1932, and viewed FDR as much less desirable. As one Boston Italian newspaper put it, "Today Roosevelt is a symbol of all that is antagonistic to the immigrant groups whereas in 1928 Al Smith was quite the opposite."

Ultimately, of course, Roosevelt did very well in 1932 in the Catholic areas of such cities as Boston, New York, and Chicago. It remained, however, to cement this into a firm partisan alliance. And the new president went out of his way to solidify Catholic support—he had Catholics in high administrative positions, cultivated urban politicians like Ed Kelly of Chicago and Frank Hague of Jersey City who had built largely Catholic-based coalitions, and even had his own clerical representatives to the American Catholic hierarchy and community.

Father John A. Ryan, for example, was head of the National Catholic Welfare Conference, a liberal, social welfare-oriented agency that engaged in informational, lobbying, and organizational activities. Ryan was fairly close to Roosevelt and quite supportive of the New Deal generally. He was in a pivotal position to defend both from charges of "communism," and so on, and to argue in return that they were very much in the spirit of modern Catholicism. He also served to coordinate Roman Catholicism with national liberal organizations, and to explain and defend the New Deal to the national Catholic community.

This was facilitated, generally, by trends in the church that seemed to justify the New Deal. Pius XI's *Quadragesimo Anno* in 1931 had moderately endorsed social reform, at least to the extent that liberals like Ryan could argue that the New Deal was a moderate and mainstream activity. Certainly the encyclical's call to lay participation in social melioration was very useful to New Deal Catholics and their supporters. And in America, church leaders had been calling since 1930 for government action against unemployment and privation, and had been criticizing business for its intemperance and lack of charity. Thus, in addition to more basic issue considerations, there were philosophical factors that also facilitated Roman Catholic Democratic support.

Probably the greatest political challenge confronting the New Deal in the Catholic context came from Father Coughlin and his potential as a spoiler in the 1936 election. Roosevelt treaded lightly concerning Coughlin from the start, realizing that he did have millions of followers, most of whom had voted Democratic in 1932. But Coughlin was a hard man to placate; he was more radical than the New Deal, in both his left-wing and his right-wing stages. He was also a prima donna and perhaps insatiably power hungry. As he grew increasingly abusive of the New Deal in 1935 and 1936, the volume of critical congressional and White House mail, especially from Irish-and German-Americans, increased appreciably.

Despite the success and popularity of New Deal programs, and the criticism of Coughlin by New Deal supporters like Father Ryan, Coughlin's appeal remained strong. Especially before Huey Long's death the spectre of his throwing in with the Louisiana senator seemed to threat-en New Deal Catholic support. Fortunately for Roosevelt, the threat diminished considerably in 1936; Coughlin's extremism and increasing anti-semitism, his alliance with Gerald L. K. Smith, and the continuing criticism of his movement by leading Catholics all helped override his strength. And his role in the Union Party of 1936 was obviously as un-successful in the outcome as it had been crucial at the beginning.

Roman Catholics, especially those who were urban, blue collar and/or recent immigrants became a mainstay of the New Deal coalition. The same was true for Jews. The latter, along with blacks, made the most complete vote shift of probably any American group; it started in 1928 and was completed by about 1936. And by the end of the 1930s it is possible that as many as 90 percent of American Jews were voting for Roosevelt, and not too many fewer considered themselves members of the Democratic party.

The reasons for their switch were pretty much the same as those for other groups, only perhaps it was more significant to them than to most others. Liberal domestic policies and an activist foreign policy cor-responded well to Jewish ambitions and needs. Moreover, the new urban Democratic party offered greater recognition to Jews than they had ever before received in American politics. The 1930s saw Jewish governors in two of the largest states in the nation. There were two Jewish Supreme Court Justices, and Jews were included among Roose-velt's foremost advisers and administrators. All this was duly noted, by Roosevelt's critics (who spoke of "the Jew Deal") and by the American Jewish community. Jews became the Democratic coalition group whose political behavior was most immune to class distinctions. While the wealthy among the Irish and other generally Democratic groups tended to move into the Republican ranks, this was not true for Jews, in the 1930s or later. This, along with their high level of participation in vot-ing and politics generally, and their concentrated living patterns, made them a more important part of the New Deal coalition than their over-all numbers would suggest.

We can seek further insight into these working class and ethnic con-stituents of the new Democratic party with another table, which also divides social characteristics into categories of high and low, by county, and compares county levels of Democratic voting (Table 3.4). The fig-ures do reinforce the idea of New Deal support coming from the poor-er, less well-educated, more foreign, more urban working class elements of the population in the northeastern quarter of the country. Just as

TABLE 3.4

Democratic Vote of Counties High and Low in Selected Social Characteristics, Urban Northeast[a]

(Percent Democratic)

		1930 Cong.	1932 Pres.	1932 Cong.	1934 Cong.	1936 Pres.	1936 Cong.	1938 Cong.
Pop./ square mile	LOW	42	50	48	50	57	52	45
	HIGH	64	68	68	64	66	71	54
Percent urban	LOW	29	44	43	46	51	48	38
	HIGH	44	51	50	51	58	54	46
Percent foreign stock	LOW	40	46	46	49	57	53	44
	HIGH	44	53	51	52	57	54	46
Percent age 18–20 in school	LOW	43	55	52	54	65	60	54
	HIGH	44	51	50	51	57	53	45
Percent unemployed 1930	LOW	44	50	49	51	56	53	45
	HIGH	39	53	51	54	62	57	50
Percent unemployed 1937	LOW	26	33	32	42	46	44	31
	HIGH	42	55	52	50	61	57	49

[a]See Appendix for description of statistics, data, and methods.

county-level data kept the correlation coefficients used earlier in this chapter rather low, so too does it result in rather modest differences here, in a statistical measure that is very gross anyway. But it makes up in clarity for its lack of precision, showing what the correlation tables sometimes masked. And the fact that each of these variables does argue in the same direction is significant.

In other regions of the country the social characteristics of the population were of course not the same. One factor, the percentage of the population aged 18 to 20 that was still in school, seems to have operated similarly everywhere but in the south. In the rural midwest and in the mountain states, for example, those in the lower category on this variable voted even more heavily Democratic relative to those in the upper category than in the urban northeast. I think this variable is a pretty good measure nationally of the breaking point between the upper middle class and everything below it, and demonstrates the relatively more feeble attraction of the Democrats to the former regardless of region or other factors.

In the mountain states, the higher category old stock showed lower Democratic averages; conversely, the higher category foreign stock showed higher Democratic voting, but only slightly. But this was not the case in the midwest farmbelt, where the large numbers of German, Swedish, and other settlers seem not to have made the same party switch as their urban cousins. On the whole, the higher old stock and lower foreign stock categories had the highest Democratic vote, with an interesting exception noted earlier: congressional and presidential voting were quite opposite (Table 3.5).

There is more than one reason for this congressional/presidential divergence, including the presence of third parties in the area. But at least part of it is due to a general popularity Roosevelt, and even aspects of the New Deal had for the foreign stock residents of this region. This popularity, reflected in their voting for Roosevelt in 1932 and 1936, simply did not transfer to a Democratic party loyalty as happened in other parts of the country. Republican tradition remained quite strong, and asserted itself in congressional elections when the famous Roosevelt presence was less felt, permitting older and more localistic forces to have prime sway.

We might profitably switch to a more direct focus on the rural population of the United States and try to find what factors or characteristics influenced the extent to which farmers did or did not join the New Deal coalition.

It was not as easy to formulate a policy to deal with and please the farmers as it was for the industrial workers, simply because farmers were a more variegated group, with many different needs and problems. The agribusinesses in the south and west, for example, were large, often diversified enterprises, which happened to specialize in agriculture; their owners were hardly "farmers" as such, but they were intimately concerned with national farm policy as well as related foreign policy and

TABLE 3.5

Democratic Voting of Counties with Higher and Lower Proportions of Foreign Stock, Nonurban Midwest[a]

(Percent Democratic)

		1930 Cong.	1932 Pres.	1932 Cong.	1934 Cong.	1936 Pres.	1936 Cong.	1938 Cong.
Old stock	LOW	25	70	30	27	60	28	20
	HIGH	45	59	54	52	53	50	47
Foreign stock	LOW	47	60	56	52	54	51	48
	HIGH	18	67	30	34	60	31	24

[a]See Appendix for description of statistics, data, and methods.

other factors. The independent farmer-businessmen who raised their own substantial crop for cash sale comprised another large and distinctive group; they corresponded to the idealized picture of the "American farmer," but had in fact already suffered economic difficulties in the 1920s and were really hurting in the Depression. Then there were the more subsistence-oriented small farmers around the country, the truck gardeners, and so on, down to the lowest and poorest farm laborers, who were found everywhere, and farm tenants and sharecroppers found mainly in the south.

Confronting this variety, which was not only economic but also, often, social and cultural, the New Deal actually had not one but several "farm problems" to deal with. It tried a number of approaches, as we have seen, but the key to its solution was in the first and second Agricultural Adjustment Acts. This was an approach that maintained the traditional focus on free enterprise or capitalistic agriculture, but in a planned and controlled way. New Deal policymakers in agriculture argued that reality was a world of big businesses, and unless farmers— through voluntary agreements or other means—made themselves big enough to be competitive they would inevitably fail, to be replaced entirely by agribusiness. Since the New Deal, like previous administrations, had an economic and ideological commitment to the national value of the family farm, much effort was expended at resolving this problem, and the AAA was the answer.

The idea of institutionalized planning was new to agriculture, and could not have been presented to a less persuadable group; American farmers were individualistic and their values were quite traditional. Thus, despite their economic problems, which were very real, they tended to be highly suspicious of this new farm bureaucracy and of centralized controls on their activities. Price supports they favored, but the mechanism chosen—production controls—they didn't like at all. Farmers were, after all, the population group in America that had most consistently, for the longest time, been used to national government support of one kind or another; many were not altogether sure that the New Deal's approach was such a good idea.

In one sense, farmers responded to the problems of Depression just as workers did—they organized. Farm organizations varied from the very radical, such as the Farm Holiday Association which ultimately tried to keep prices up through physically halting the flow of goods to market in the worst days of the Depression; to the more pragmatic, such as the American Farm Bureau Federation, which grew rapidly in these years, coming to represent 450,000 member families by the end of the decade; to the oligopolistic, as in the case of agribusiness cartels in the west. And beyond this, farmers were not only farmers, not just economic actors; they very often had real social, ethnic, and religious commitments that also influenced their reactions to national affairs.

New Deal policy in the end did not please very many farmers. This was not because it was an entirely unsuccessful policy; indeed, most farmers did improve their economic positions as a result of it. But many did not improve as much as they had hoped, others simply expected too much, and still others were ultimately unwilling to make the sacrifice of accepting big government and outside control regardless of the economic advantage. To many farmers, in fact, it seemed more and more that the New Deal was a political movement of the cities and for the cities—they resented the money going to labor and urban people generally, often for cultural and ideological reasons rather than purely economic ones. Thus, the Democrat's honeymoon with most farmers was not a very long one, but there were exceptions, small in some areas, larger in others.

Table 3.6, for example, shows the relative diffidence of the midwest farmbelt's flirtation with the Democratic party. Farmbelt counties were slow to rise to the Democrats in the early Depression, and never made a partisan commitment to the Democrats at the congressional level. The nonurban mountain states, on the other hand, which were more

TABLE 3.6

Average County Democratic Vote for Selected Regions[a]

(Percent Democratic)

	Urban Northeast	Nonurban Midwest	Nonurban Mountain	Nonurban South
1930 Congress	43	36	48	92
1932 President	51	62	60	87
1932 Congress	49	48	56	89
1934 Congress	51	47	63	94
1936 President	57	56	64	85
1936 Congress	54	45	62	90
1938 Congress	46	40	56	96

[a]Each county given equal weight. See Appendix for description of statistics, data, and methods.

mixed in their economic characteristics (farming, ranching, mining, etc.) made a more dramatic switch and held it through the decade. And the rural south simply maintained a traditionally overwhelming commitment to the Democrats.

Finally, Table 3.7 examines three more variables and their suggested influence in the three nonurban regions. For the midwest and mountain states, counties lower in percent rural farm (i.e., with more of their population in towns) voted somewhat more Democratic, and this was increasingly true over time. The more purely farming areas seem to have lost some of their enthusiasm for the New Deal more quickly. The same does not hold true for the overwhelmingly Democratic south; indeed the difference becomes almost nil later in the decade.

On the other hand, farm tenancy can be seen once again as appar-

TABLE 3.7

Democratic Voting of Counties with Varying Proportions of Agricultural Characteristics[a]

(Percent Democratic)

		1930 Cong.	1932 Pres.	1932 Cong.	1934 Cong.	1936 Pres.	1936 Cong.	1938 Cong.
		Nonurban Midwest						
Percent rural farm	LOW	37	56	50	52	58	48	44
	HIGH	33	65	46	42	53	41	37
Percent farms tenanted	LOW	13	56	23	24	69	17	18
	HIGH	32	66	54	60	60	50	48
Mean farm acres	100–512	44	60	57	58	63	58	53
	512–5000	37	62	48	48	56	44	40
	5000+	34	63	46	46	55	46	40
		Nonurban South						
Percent rural farm	LOW	89	79	80	94	81	87	94
	HIGH	94	89	91	94	86	90	96
Percent farms tenanted	LOW	84	71	67	84	60	94	89
	HIGH	96	94	96	99	92	97	99
Mean farm acres	0–100	91	72	63	91	80	77	98
	100–512	92	86	87	95	86	77	98
	512–5000	91	87	89	93	85	90	95
	5000+	91	87	91	99	86	95	99

TABLE 3.7 (cont'd)

		1930 Cong.	1932 Pres.	1932 Cong.	1934 Cong.	1936 Pres.	1936 Cong.	1938 Cong.
		Nonurban Mountain						
Percent rural farm	LOW	53	62	59	66	68	66	63
	HIGH	40	58	49	60	59	55	50
Percent farms tenanted	LOW	49	59	56	63	64	63	59
	HIGH	47	60	56	63	63	62	55
Mean farm acres	512–5000	45	59	56	62	63	64	58
	5000+	50	61	56	63	64	61	55

[a]See Appendix for description of statistics, data, and methods.

parently quite influential in voting. This is true in the south, where I have already noted the apparent affinity of tenants for the Democrats. And it is even more striking in the midwest—except for the presidential contest of 1936—and suggests that here, too, this poorest element of the rural population was most attracted to the New Deal. The figures do not indicate much in the mountain states, mainly because of the relatively low number of tenant farmers in the area.

These variables suggest the inverse relationship between wealth and Democratic voting that is generally characteristic of the rise of the New Deal coalition. And for the midwest, this is reinforced by the data on average farm acres. Counties with higher proportions of their farms under 500 acres voted appreciably more Democratic than those with larger farms, and this remained quite constant over time. Differences between counties with average farm sizes of 512–5000, as against those over 5000 acres, were very slight, but nonetheless consistent. In the mountain states, where all farms tended to be larger, voting differences were very slight. And in the south (where there were, in fact, very few counties with average farm acres below 100) the measure is not consistent with the other two variables; I do not know why the counties with smaller farms are distinctly lower in Democratic voting on three occasions.

Overall, the more intensively agricultural an area was, the more likely was its attraction to the New Deal to be short-lived. Farm poverty, especially as expressed by the presence of tenancy, seems to have been highly related with voting Democratic, as was the ownership of smaller farms in the midwest. This suggests, again, that those who were most poor in farming areas—tenants on farms and various kinds of workers in the towns and small cities—joined their class brothers in urban areas in moving toward and staying with the Democrats. Farmers joined the Democratic coalition not as farmers, per se, but on the basis of their poverty and, perhaps, other characteristics.

One of the most dramatic and far-reaching popular political shifts of the New Deal years was among black voters. Following Frederick Douglass' famous dictum, "The Republican party is the ship, all else is open sea," blacks who were outside the south and thus able to vote continued the commitment to the party of Lincoln that had begun with emancipation. In Chicago, for example, during the 1920s, the black Democratic presidential vote never exceeded 23 percent; and in 1920 and 1924 it was only about ten percent. This was not unusual for northern black voting, and it tended to be pretty much the same for state and local politics as well.

Roosevelt won without the black vote in 1932; he received about 21 percent of the black vote in Chicago, a bit more in border areas like Knoxville and Cincinnati, but nowhere did blacks evince any great interest in the Democratic party. And this was despite the fact that few groups were hurting as badly from the Depression as were blacks. They tended to have the most disposable types of jobs, resulting in enormous unemployment by 1933. Not only were they in relatively insecure jobs, they were also less likely to be union members (24 international unions in New York excluded blacks entirely as late as 1936) and have whatever security came from such membership.

In 1930 still over one-half of the black population lived in rural areas, mainly in the south. And less than 20 percent of black farmers owned their land. Thus a large part of the black population included tenant farmers and farm laborers, a group that had been poor before the Depression and fared very badly with it. Moreover, southern racism meant that what little relief activity southern states did engage in was not very likely to be apportioned on a nonracial basis.

In the northern cities, blacks were losing jobs and being added to relief rolls twice as frequently, proportionately, as others; and they were finding new jobs one-half as frequently as whites. In Chicago, for example, one-half of the black domestic servants, one-third of the semi-skilled and one-fourth of the unskilled were unemployed in 1935. Indeed, in that year perhaps as much as one-half of the nation's black population was in need of relief of one kind or another. These problems were steadily exacerbated as thousands of southern blacks continued the migration northward during the depression years; they were fleeing a known poverty for an unknown one.

New Deal and Democratic party leaders were impressed with the magnitude of these problems and of the black commitment to Republicanism. From an idealistic standpoint, New Dealers like Harold Ickes, who had been very active in the NAACP, and Eleanor Roosevelt wanted to use the New Deal to upgrade at least the economic aspect of black lives in America, and if possible to affect social and other conditions as well. The politicians, like Farley and the president himself, wanted to bring blacks into the Democratic coalition, but not at the expense of the south; we have already seen how sensitive Roosevelt was to this issue.

Thus the New Deal approach to questions of race, and of the application of general programs irrespective of race, was indirect, often painfully halting, and inconsistent. The preponderant employment of blacks in agriculture and household service, for example, meant that large numbers of them were in occupational areas for which there were no NRA codes; likewise the Wagner Act would affect them less than other groups because they were in occupations much less likely to be organized.

These were not insoluble problems, however, when the will was there. Ickes, as head of the Public Works Administration, for example, insisted that some of the contracted jobs go to unemployed blacks; he also insisted that black schools and hospitals be built along with white ones; and under his control fully one-third of the public housing built by the New Deal was for black occupation. Harry Hopkins of the WPA acted similarly: blacks received a share of WPA and FERA funds greater than their proportion of the population; it is estimated that as much as 40 percent of the American black population was receiving relief of some kind—often very minimal—in 1935.

The attitude of individual administrators was often crucial. The CCC, for example, showed little sympathy for blacks. But the National Youth Administration, under Aubrey Williams, had more blacks in its administrative apparatus than did any other New Deal program, and its programs served many blacks as well.

All of these programs were not without imperfections in their attempted inclusion of blacks. There was popular obstructionism, administrative racism, and so on. But this was primarily true in the south, where things were generally not administered fairly, but where also there was little the New Dealers could do. Southern blacks fared less well vis-à-vis the New Deal than southern whites, or northern blacks, and that is one reason why the stream of northward migration continued strong throughout the decade.

In the administration of the Agricultural Adjustment Act, for example, New Deal administrators were most anxious to see their controversial and complicated program work. Thus, they did not really protest the exclusion of blacks from the huge administrative procedure set up by the legislation; not one black served on a single county committee throughout the south. Local control was a key element in making the AAA acceptable to farmers; and local control meant black exclusion. When the second AAA tried to deal more directly with the problems of black tenant farmers in 1936–1938 it met tremendous landlord opposition and gave in.

On the other hand, blacks did vote, at federal insistence, in AAA administrative elections—a small thing, in its way, but not insignificant in areas where blacks had not been permitted to vote for over a generation. And blacks received about one-fourth of the loans made by the Farm Security Administration in the south to permit tenants to purchase their own land at low rates; it was not a large program, but showed areas in which the federal government could act to aid blacks without endangering southern white support for the administration.

Beyond this, the New Deal did little relative to distinctly social problems. No civil rights legislation was passed, the administration abandoned the anti-lynching bill to avoid losing southern congressional support, and even the minimum wage and maximum hours law was compromised in ways to minimize its potential effect on the subservience of black people in the south. In terms of appointments and general recognition, the New Deal did better. More blacks were appointed to prestigious and significant government positions in the Roosevelt administration than ever before. This was important in a symbolic way, and also practically—in providing a cadre of new black leaders who could push for even greater change.

And while Roosevelt personally insisted on staying out of racial issues, he was not averse to seeing New Dealers like Ickes become known as leading civil rights activists. The same held true for his wife's role, as in her famous resignation from the Daughters of the American Revolution when it refused to permit singer Marian Anderson to perform in its hall. It was Eleanor Roosevelt and Harold Ickes who arranged that she sing, instead, from the steps of the Lincoln Memorial.

All of these things were important, as were the activities of the professional politicians in the New Deal. Despite the fear of alienating the south, blacks comprised too large a group for national and local New Deal politicians like Farley, Joseph Guffey, and Mayor Kelly to ignore, especially as the proportions of blacks in northern cities grew increasingly impressive.

It was Guffey, of Pennsylvania, who pressured Farley and Howe to set up a "Negro Division" for the 1932 campaign; likewise he persuaded Roosevelt to name Robert L. Vann, publisher of the *Pittsburgh Courier,* as Assistant to the Attorney General, the highest federal office yet achieved by a black and a sign of things to come. Guffey had also made an agreement of sorts with Pennsylvania blacks that they would get exactly ten percent of Pennsylvania patronage, and equity in relief, and so on, if they supported the Democrats. The New York Democrats, the Pendergast machine in Kansas City, and others emulated Guffey.

Robert L. Vann did switch his newspaper's political loyalty in 1932, and tried to persuade other black leaders to do the same. One New Jersey Republican leader complained that "The Negro newspapers have deserted us." But a political commitment as deep as that of blacks to the Republican party would not change overnight. Roosevelt in 1932 picked up quite a few black leaders who were already critical of Republican general neglect and Hoover administration Depression policies, and some voters, but not really very many of the latter.

Black leaders were watching the New Deal after 1932, and were increasingly impressed, not by any civil rights action, per se, but by the extent to which blacks were, relatively speaking, represented in the administration, and also the ways in which blacks generally profited from New Deal programs. By 1936 the new National Negro Congress held its first general convention in Chicago. The leadership was by no means united, ranging from business-oriented and thus anti-New Deal conservatives like Robert S. Abbott of the *Chicago Defender,* to, at the other end, A. Phillip Randolph and Ralph Bunche who criticized the New Deal from the Socialist left. But it was obvious at least that the long marriage to the Republicans was over; and many at the meeting were by now committed Democrats and New Dealers, a position that suddenly was not as strange as one would have thought a few years before.

Perhaps a better indication of all this can be seen among a more practical group: black politicians. These office-holders and would-be office-holders had every reason to try to anticipate objectively the direction of the political sympathies of their constituents in the near term. Sometimes this was clearer at the local level—where rewards and punishments came more quickly and numerously—than at the national, but nonetheless it began to emerge.

In Chicago, for example, Oscar DePriest had become in 1928 the first northern black congressman in history; he was, of course, a Republican. But in 1934 an ambitious black politician named Arthur W. Mitchell was slated by the Democrats against him, and despite the lack of influential support (the *Chicago Defender* stayed with DePriest) he won the district, becoming the first black Democrat ever to serve in Congress. The combination of the rising popularity and power of the Democrats, along with the slating of black candidates, was influential indeed. Between 1934 and 1938 more and more erstwhile black Republicans, looking to long political careers, made the switch. Again in Chicago, this was the case with William L. Dawson, who had started his career as a Republican, but began his long congressional tenure as a Democrat in 1938. The successful leader was one who could anticipate where his followers would want to go.

It is impossible to see the effects of the black vote in county level data, but we can look at one or more cities to get an idea of what was happening. Table 3.8 gives the Democratic percentage of the vote of the key black areas of Chicago during 1928 to 1936. I have included a couple of mayoral contests to show that the switch involved local as

TABLE 3.8

Black Voting in Chicago 1928–1936[a]

	1928 President	1931 Mayor	1932 President	1935 Mayor	1936 President
Percent democratic	23	16	21	72	45

[a]Source: J. M. Allswang, "The Chicago Negro Voter and the Democratic Consensus," *Ill. State Hist. Soc. Journal* (Summer, 1967).

well as national politics. And, indeed, for Chicago the switch was not complete by 1936 by any means. The completion of the black Democratic shift at all levels—local, state, national—would come in the 1938 congressional and 1940 presidential contests in Chicago, but the direction was already quite clear by 1936, and was reinforced by black responses to public opinion polls, as cited above.

The process was the same for most northern cities, although the timing varied a bit. In Cincinnati, for example, the city's most black ward went from 29 percent Democratic for president in 1932, to 65 percent Democratic in 1936. In the two most black wards in Knoxville, Roosevelt also took fairly strong majorities (67% and 56%) in 1936, after running way behind Hoover in 1932. But whatever the city, by the end of the second Roosevelt administration northern black voters had made a complete, and quite logical, shift in their traditional partisan loyalties, one that would be extremely unremitting and longlasting. This shift, combined with the steadily increasing black populations in northern cities from that time forward, brought in one of the single most important parts of the New Deal coalition.

Another way to seek understanding of the popular political effects of the New Deal is to work backwards—to try to isolate the main sources of opposition to the Democrats during the 1930s. Here once again the increasing class base of American politics is apparent. Certainly part of this division preceded Roosevelt; at least outside of the south and especially in the cities, the different social bases of the two parties were becoming more apparent in 1920s. But the policies of the New Deal vis-à-vis the Depression intensified this division: wealthy Democrats and unwealthy Republicans voted so consistently against their party traditions that, with time, they can be said to have made membership switches.

In one of the early Gallup Polls, in January 1936, two samples were asked if they preferred the reelection of President Roosevelt or his replacement with a Republican. In the national sample, 53 percent preferred the president; but in the sample of listees in *Who's Who,* only 31 percent were pro-Roosevelt. This is a small indication of the overwhelming opposition people of wealth and position developed toward Roosevelt, the New Deal, and, ultimately, the Democratic party. As columnist Marquis Childs pointed out in an article in 1936, the hatred for Roosevelt by the upper middle and upper classes could in no way be explained purely in economic terms. Indeed, business in the long run profited from the new state control of the economy. But the New Deal, and Roosevelt personally and especially, seemed to also signify the end of traditional authority in America, the identification and defeat of its traditional ruling class by the masses, led by upper class traitors like the president. Roosevelt was hated, as well as loved, probably more deeply than any chief executive in the nation's history.

This is most clearly seen in the rise of the American Liberty League, the chief effort of the elite of American business and society to reverse the course of history in the 1930s. A famous exchange of letters between two men who would be Liberty League activists is illustrative. R. R. M. Carpenter, an executive DuPont, wrote to John J. Raskob in 1934 that "Five negroes [sic] on my place in South Carolina refused to work this spring . . . saying they had easy jobs with the government. . . . A cook on my houseboat at Fort Myers quit because the government was paying him a dollar an hour as a painter." Raskob responded sympathetically, pointing out the need for industry to organize and to fight the implications of "communistic elements . . . that all business-men are crooks." The people had to be encouraged to work, which was not what the government was doing at all.

These sentiments suggest several things. The New Deal was not simply economically wrong, but it was socially revolutionary and dangerous. It was disrupting the natural order of things, and in an evil direction. People were losing their sense of place, which was dangerous indeed. Moreover, government was becoming too big and too involved in the lives and affairs of the American people; this was undercutting traditional values and class relationships. Finally, the economic danger was real—in government spending, in too high wages to workers, in the undermining of capitalism.

The legislation of the second Hundred Days removed any doubt that some business people and upper class Americans may have had about the reality of these dangers. The National Labor Relations Act, and its resultant great organizing drives and assertiveness of workers, was a key element. Corporation lawyers, reflecting the earlier success of court invalidation of the NIRA and the AAA, advised their clients to reject NLRB decisions and take them to court. The Liberty League, the National Association of Manufacturers, and other groups aided in the tests of constitutionality. When one United States Steel vice president told the American Management Association in 1935 that, rather than obey the NLRA he would "go to jail or be convicted as a felon," he expressed common sentiments among his peers.

The American Liberty League was ostensibly nonpartisan and not anti-FDR, but of course the opposite was the case. It was created as a political action agency of business and social leaders to defeat Roosevelt and the Democrats in 1936. It was chartered in the District of Columbia in 1934 to "teach the necessity of respect for the rights of property . . . and . . . the duty of government to encourage and protect individual and group initiatives and enterprises." Its leaders came primarily from the executives of General Motors and DuPont.

It is interesting that the Liberty League's ultimate origins were in the Association Against the Prohibition Amendment, a 1920s business group, also including people like Raskob and the Duponts, which had opposed Prohibition on economic grounds. They had been quite successful overall, and had obtained considerable influence in the Democratic party; Raskob had been made Democratic National Chairman by Al Smith in 1928. Thus, among other things, the rise of the New Deal meant that the relatively new influence that these industrial leaders, largely Roman Catholic, had developed in the Democratic party had also come to an end. Of the six members of the American Liberty League's Administrative Committee, five had been leaders of the Association Against the Prohibition Amendment.

At the outset, Liberty League leaders anticipated a broad-based movement, with millions of supporters from all areas of society; farmer and labor divisions were planned. But this was simply a measure of how out of touch with the realities of American society these people actually were. It remained throughout an elite movement, never numbering more than the approximately 125,000 members it had during the 1936 presidential campaign. Moreover, it was active primarily in the industrial states, and large parts of the country only read about it, vaguely, in their newspapers and magazines.

The American Liberty League was strikingly unsuccessful in challenging the most popular president and administration in modern American history. Despite the support of some previously influential conservative Democrats, like Al Smith and Raskob, it served only to influence Republicans, and even then a great deal less than its leaders had anticipated.

They certainly tried, however. Twelve members of the DuPont family alone contributed over $620,000 to the 1936 campaign. And five members of the Pew family in Philadelphia added more than $300,000. Thus, these two families alone contributed more in 1936 than the whole labor movement—to opposite sides, obviously—but to very little avail.

Campaign contributions are themselves an interesting indication of political allegiance and aspiration. In 1936, for example, the Republican National Committee spent $8.9 million compared with $5.6 million by the Democrats; the Republican state party committees had another $4.5 million, with $2.7 million for the Democrats. The Republicans thus spent 85¢ per vote, while the Democrats spent only 33¢ per vote— American business leadership got a bad bargain in 1936.

There were some significant changes between 1932 and 1936 concerning contributions over one thousand dollars. The Democrats had gotten 33 percent of their money in the former year from "Bankers, Brokers and Manufacturers." This was halved to 17 percent in 1936. On the other hand, labor supplied at least ten percent of the Democrat's funds for that year, and zero to the Republicans. "Bankers, Brokers and Manufacturers" provided 44 percent of Republican money in 1936.

The Democratic alliance with labor was very important, producing the highest Democratic campaign fund totals in history. Labor spent almost $800,000 (funds it would never had had were it not for the steady increase in number and size of unions during the decade), which it distributed for a wide variety of national, state, and local races.

Another indication of business opposition to the Democrats was seen in the party's lack of media support. Newspapers tend to be business-oriented, sometimes business-dependent, and big newspapers are big businesses. Moreover, newspapers saw themselves as victims of New Deal legislation. The NIRA codes included one for newspapers, and the labor legislation augured ill for the profits of publishers. Col. Robert R. McCormick of the *Chicago Tribune,* an old friend of Roosevelt, was infuriated at the NIRA newspaper code, criticizing its minimum wage and maximum hour provisions as attacks on freedom of the press, with penury among reporters and other workers apparently being a key to journalistic integrity. McCormick would be among those who epitomized FDR personally as a sign of the evils of the New Deal, and who hated him as a traitor to his class. William Randolph Hearst had long been involved in Democratic and liberal causes; he owned twenty-eight newspapers with 5.5 million weekday readers, plus features he sold to 2000 other publications. The rise of the Newspaper Guild in 1934–1935 severely tested his liberalism, to the point that he changed his politics and had all his papers working hard to defeat Roosevelt in 1936.

Wealth and privilege, therefore, were quite strongly united against the New Deal by 1936, and made a major exception to the generality of the new Democratic coalition. On the whole they would remain out of it permanently, and in so doing provide one of the confident ways in which that coalition could be defined.

The middle class, on the other hand, is less easy to categorize politically. It was large, amorphous, and varied economically, ethnically, and otherwise. But most middle class Americans held neither the great wealth nor the lofty and endangered social position that was so important to DuPonts and McCormicks. Moreover, much of the New Deal program had direct middle class appeal: they, too, suffered unemployment, failing mortgages, white collar exploitation, and so on.

One middle class salesman well expressed the ways in which the New Deal affected his own group: "I am a salesman in a chain store. Before NRA I worked 7 AM to 10 or 11 PM. Now two of us work eight hours a day each. If they don't extend NRA one of us gets fired and the other works 14 or 15 hours." A southern shopgirl lectured an interviewer on social security, "We call it human security and we all know about it." She was adamant about its maintenance, and knew where it came from.

A convenient example of the nature of class response to the New Deal, and thus to the Democratic party, can be seen in an analysis of 1000 letters sent to the office of the Solicitor General, Robert H. Jackson: "If the letter had been dictated on lithographed or engraved stationery, the chances were about 75 to 25 that it opposed the administration. If it had been personally pecked out on a typewriter, the chances of criticism or support were about 50-50. . . . But, if the letter had been written in pencil and on tablet paper, the chances were about 99 to 1 that the writer was a staunch supporter of the Administration."

There were noneconomic, nonclass bases for opposition to the New Deal as well, but they tend to be less clear, more regional, and highly selective. One such influential force was ethnic. The real or apparent concern of the New Deal for recent immigrants, Jews, and blacks, and the demonstrably increased position and influence of these groups in national politics and Democratic party positions were offensive to many. This included extreme groups like the German-American (Nazi) Bund, and much more conventional ones like upper middle class Americans who had never liked Jews or other minorities ("You kiss the Negores/I'll kiss the Jews/And we'll stay in the White House/As long as we choose"). The potential rise of blacks via the New Deal was threatening to many, although it still seemed remote and tangential. But the Jewish threat was real—on the Supreme Court (even two at a time!), in the highest councils of government and politics, increasingly as holders of major public office. The New Deal seemed to many old stock Americans not only Jewish in personnel, but also, somehow, in philosophy, particularly in its more radical aspects. Because the Jews were identified as both the leaders of international socialism and, at the same time, the crux of capitalist reaction, they were useful to all sides, and often stigmatized as the key evil behind the changes of the New Deal.

I think it is in these social and cultural phenomena that one finds the best explanation for rural and small town opposition to the Democrats by the period 1936-1938, and their weak alliances with the Democratic coalition from that time forward. The Democrat's farm policy was not unattractive, nor were the wide variety of other domestic reforms. But there seemed to be an alien kind of general change, seen in part in the kind of people who were in power, in part in the increasing power of government programs, in part in an unrationalized reaction to the fact that some aspects of modern life had pretty much passed by rural and small town people. Given this, they held on to their traditional values—values that they could afford to maintain only because those in Washington had given them up to support rural America while it increasingly condemned its benefactor.

Outside of the one-party south by the end of the second Hundred Days, there was an unconscious consensus developing among some Americans that whatever the economic advantages the New Deal had brought (and even these seemed more arguable in the 1937-1938 recession), they had been at too great cost. Traditional values were being sacrificed, individual privacy and freedom of action had diminished, collectivism and "governmentism" were triumphant, social and cultural and ethnic unrest were threatening traditional balances among people. This phenomenon was clearest in the rural and small town areas, where the largest number of susceptible people lived, but it was also found elsewhere—in the cities to which members of the susceptible groups had been coming for a generation. These groups, along with the upper and upper middle class business and professional leadership, would be the mainstay of the Republican party from New Deal times forward; as it turned out, they were too few in numbers—their fears had been quite rational, the country had been largely taken away from them.

I have specifically excluded the popular mass movements of the early New Deal years from mention in this section on the foes of the New Deal because they were, in effect, really political forces operating on the New Deal, not effects of or reactions to it. Huey Long's Share

Our Wealth movement, Father Charles Coughlin's National Union for Social Justice, and Dr. Frances Townsend's Old Age Revolving Pensions, Ltd., while appealing to different groups on somewhat different bases, all drew their strength from the realities of the Depression in 1933-1935, and their regional and cultural effects. Huey Long was the only one of the three with real political flair, and his national rather than regional political viability was never to be tested because of his assassination in 1935.

That these movements were important only in influencing the direction of the New Deal in 1934-1936, and not in any independent way, was made most clear in the 1936 elections. Coughlin, Townsend, and Gerald L. K. Smith (Long's successor, who would, like Coughlin, prove his own instability by moving from the left to the far right, becoming a fascist) did unite behind the Union party. But that party was essentially in the tradition of farm rebellion, as was its standard-bearer, William Lemke. Lemke, a former Republican, became the candidate largely through the efforts of Father Coughlin; and the choice reflected the very limited options really available to Coughlin, Smith, et al. in 1936.

The Union Party was essentially negative, running against Roosevelt and the New Deal. It's whole position was one of opposition to the New Deal, and Roosevelt personally, offering little in terms of program other than Lemke's own inflationary beliefs. Its supporters were too disparate to permit firm positions.

More important was the fact that the party did very poorly. It was never able to develop a real national organization, nor could it get financing; the Liberty League, for example, with its great wealth, followed the path of Republicanism as the workable alternative, not a third party. Candidate Lemke wisely did not give up his nomination for return to Congress; ultimately he stopped much of his presidential campaigning so as not to lose his seat in the House.

To his credit, Lemke did not follow the path of Coughlin and Smith. He did not campaign to appeal to the haters—the anti-semites, racists, religious bigots, and so on. If he had done so, if he and others had tried to turn the Union Party into an American fascist party, they would probably have done somewhat better in 1936, but only marginally so. Neither the moderate nor the radical paths could lead them anywhere that year. And their effort had less long-range effect on American politics and voting than those of the other New Deal opponents already described.

The rise of the Democratic party to majority strength in the time of Roosevelt and the Depression was the rise of a party of mass strength on mass issues. This was its distinctive aspect, what made it somewhat different from the rise of the Republicans in the 1890s; it also helps explain why the Democrats have remained the dominant party for over forty years. Organizations were of course important, be they labor unions or ethnic and religious groups, but nonetheless the key appeal was directly to the American masses; and this was the first such coalition built—at least since Jackson, perhaps ever.

What has been called the "New Deal Party System" is an issue-oriented, group-based coalition, more so than that preceding it. Certainly it was distinctive from its Republican predecessor in both the kinds of issues stressed, and the government's position on those issues. Never before had an American government, or political party, made so clear a commitment to the social and economic problems of the American masses (not an unqualified commitment, or a total one, but relatively great nonetheless), and the political response of the masses was understandably enthusiastic.

This realignment of voters, as we have seen, took some time, and at least part of its origins (and an important part) has to be laid to national and local political developments in the 1920s, especially the alienation of the urban masses from the Republicans and the complementary attractiveness of the Smith presidential candidacy of 1928. At least one scholar has made an interesting division in the alignment theory, arguing that first there was a realignment "along ethnic and life style lines" in the late 1920s; and then another, complementary realignment "along economic lines" in 1936. This is a suggestive interpretation, especially in emphasizing these two areas of political motivation, and it has some value, particularly in explaining the basic forces of the voting changes in 1928.

However, one must beware of too facile separation of variables; the ethnic and economic greatly reinforce one another. Moreover, the data in this chapter seem to suggest that economic factors had their greatest force at the height of the Depression, especially in the election of 1932, rather than 1936. What seems more significant about 1936, and after, is the increasing importance of the variable of socioeconomic class, not just economics—and the difference between the two is very real. The ethnic/religious/cultural forces operating for the Democrats by the end of the 1920s, due to the strength of issues like Prohibition and immigration restriction, were reinforced, first, by the economic crisis of the

Depression, and later, by the increasingly class-based divisions in American society. These last emanated from lingering Depression problems, the New Deal's ambitious legislative program and its effects (the rise of the organized labor movement, especially), and the reaction of many upper-middle and upper class Americans against these new forces for reasons already discussed.

The overall effect of this was a major, even drastic shift in mass political behavior and partisan power. Whether or not the effect was complementary at state and local levels, and within national government itself, comprises additional questions we shall deal with in the next three chapters.

FOUR

The New Deal
in the Cities

We have seen in the preceding chapter that the people of the cities played a major role in the development of the New Deal coalition. Industrial, especially union, workers, immigrants, blacks by the end of the 1930s, and certainly the urban poor all were important in this political process. In this chapter I want to look at this phenomenon somewhat more closely, and also consider aspects of urban politics apart from voting per se as they were influenced by the Depression and the New Deal.

First we can look more closely at some characteristics of urban voting. Whereas this was done more generally in Chapter 3, considering as urban those counties in the northeastern quadrant of the nation that had populations in excess of 250,000 (a total of 44 counties), for this chapter we shall deal with all counties anywhere in the country with populations in excess of 500,000 people (a total of 21, to be labeled "metropolitan").

Table 4.1 compares the voting of these counties to averages of all counties and other subgroups of counties. And what is immediately apparent is a caution of sorts relative to some traditional conclusions

TABLE 4.1

Voting Patterns for Groups of Counties[a]

(Percent Democratic)

	Metro-politan	Nonurban Midwest	Nonurban Mountain	Nonurban South	National-All Counties
1930 Congress	41	36	48	92	58
1932 President	57	62	60	87	68
1932 Congress	51	48	56	89	64
1934 Congress	52	47	63	94	66
1936 President	62	56	64	85	66
1936 Congress	54	45	62	90	64
1938 Congress	46	40	56	96	63

[a]See Appendix for description of statistics, data, and methods.

about the role of the cities in the New Deal coalition. I do not mean to impugn what I have said above, but rather to offer an important qualifier: the cities and urban populations played a role *relatively* less great than is generally suggested in the 1930s rise of the Democrats. Their role was important, but no more so than that of other geographic areas and population groups. Where the cities became increasingly distinctive in Democratic partisanship and role was in the post-New Deal years, since their commitment to the party tended to remain quite constant while that of other areas did not.

Two other caveats deserve mention. One is that we often ignore the fact that for no place and no group did all the people vote unanimously. There was always in the 1930s a viable Republican presence every-

TABLE 4.2

Correlations of Elections for Metropolitan Counties[a]

(Based on Percent Democratic)

	1930 Cong.	1932 Pres.	1932 Cong.	1934 Cong.	1936 Pres.	1936 Cong.	1938 Cong.
1930 Congress	—	.345	.808	.779	−.080	.591	.649
1932 President		—	.357	.319	.749	.427	.221
1932 Congress			—	.914	.076	.720	.882
1934 Congress				—	.110	.856	.927
1936 President					—	.352	.140
1936 Congress						—	.788
1938 Congress							—

[a]Pearson's *r*. See Appendix for description of statistics, data, and methods.

where in the country except the deep south, and the same applies even more to the state voting I shall talk about in the next chapter. Although this is an obvious, almost superfluous, generalization, it is nonetheless worth making. The other is that I am dealing with county-level data, not city data as such. The city of Chicago, for example, made up 85 percent of the population of Cook County in the 1930 census year; since the noncity county was demographically quite different from the city, its voting was also different. This is only fifteen percent of the population, but it does somewhat distort the reality of the Chicago vote —not enough to invalidate the data, but still something to bear in mind. It is true for other urban counties as well.

All this can be amplified in Tables 4.2 and 4.3. Table 4.2 looks at the relationship (coefficients of correlation) of the various elections to

TABLE 4.3

Correlates of Democratic Voting for Metropolitan Counties[a]

	Percent Foreign Stock	Percent Black	Percent Age 18–20 in School	Percent Unemployed 1937
1930 Congress	.575	.002	−.521	.324
1932 President	.527	−.349	−.071	.200
1932 Congress	.446	.101	−.545	.406
1934 Congress	.467	.127	−.669	.387
1936 President	.142	−.065	−.089	.193
1936 Congress	.442	.296	−.711	.490
1938 Congress	.296	.233	−.604	.341

[a]Pearson's *r*. See Appendix for description of statistics, data, and methods.

one another for these 21 counties. Table 4.3 examines the same statistical measure of relationship between selected independent variables and the elections.

What is most striking in Table 4.2 is the separation of congressional and presidential voting; there are no strong statistical relationships between any congressional and any presidential election. On the other hand, between the two presidential races the relationship is strong, and the same holds among congressional races. The main reason for this, I think, is that, while almost everyone who voted Democratic for Congress also voted for Roosevelt, the opposite was not the case. The president's popularity certainly helped his party, but did not move everyone to his party. Partisan loyalties are simply less controlling for presidential voting than at lesser levels—a factor notably true since the

Roosevelt years, when Republican presidents have been elected amidst otherwise great Democratic enthusiasm.

On the other hand, the strong correlations among the congressional elections, especially after 1930, do show that the cities were part of this partisan development. Their intercongressional correlations were higher than those for the midwest nonurban counties, the mountain counties, and even much of the time the solid south. This suggests the solidity of the Democratic commitment of urban peoples.

Table 4.3 simply provides a comparison with the tables in Chapter 3, here focussing on the largest cities. Again, county-level data do not lead to ideal correlations. Nonetheless, compared to Table 3.2 we can see that the relationship between foreign stock and voting Democratic was highest in these big cities. And the same is true for the relationship between percent unemployed and, negatively, percentage of those aged 18 to 20 who were still in school. The jobless, the poor, the lower and working class, and the ethnic groups were indeed a key part of the urban Democratic coalition; and these groups were more likely to become part of that coalition in the big cities than anywhere else. We even have some indication of the mid-1930s switch in the black vote in these cities, in the turnaround of the low-level relationships for congressional voting in 1936 and 1938.

This popular voting change is a basic part of the effect of the Depression and the New Deal on the cities; it played an important role in turning them to the Democratic coalition, thus reinforcing the positions of new or old urban Democratic organizations. But the interrelationship of the New Deal and the cities had more dimensions than just this. One urban historian has noted that the period "marked a new epoch in American urban history" in that it comprised the first real recognition of the cities as distinct entities with distinct problems by the federal government. This recognition, plus the political importance of the cities, resulted in far greater urban access to Washington than ever before; the federal–city relationship became direct, avoiding the state intermediation that had previously been the norm.

This political relationship was clearly reciprocal. As much as Roosevelt and the New Deal helped turn urban populations permanently Democratic, so too did established Democratic city organizations like those in New York, Boston, and Chicago play a key role in the president's and the party's initial electoral success. For every Philadelphia, whose deep Republicanism was turned around between 1932 and 1934 via New Deal programs, jobs, and money, there was a Jersey City whose local Democratic strength facilitated the party's rise to national power.

Roosevelt had traditionally been somewhat suspicious of big cities. He considered himself (and in attitude really was) a nonurban man. As late as his gubernatorial years he continued to show more concern, perhaps even more compassion, for rural people and problems than for urban ones; and during the 1932 campaign he confessed to one of his staff that he had a hard time relating to "city people." This was understandable, not only due to his genteel Duchess County background, but also to his political career: as a moderate reformer in New York state politics he had often enough run afoul of Tammany Hall, its politics and its interests. It had even affected his career when he ran for the U. S. Senate in 1914 despite the lack of an endorsement from Tammany leader Charles Francis Murphy; Murphy's man beat him in the primary.

But Roosevelt would become aware of and concerned with the cities quickly enough. The reasons were both political, as we shall see, and more straightforward—many of the most grueling economic and social problems he was committed to dealing with were really focussed there. Much of the earliest insistence for federal government activism, directed first to Hoover and then to FDR, came from the mayors, who were bearing the brunt of urban discontent and desperation. State governors, and, even more, rural-dominated state legislatures, were not very sympathetic, certainly not to the point of providing the levels of relief spending required. And traditional organizations like the National Municipal League were held captive by their own traditions; they were not devised, nor could they reorient themselves, to deal with problems like the Great Depression.

Thus, the mayors, who were on the political firing line, became more militant, better organized, more adamant. Leaders like Frank Murphy, elected mayor of Detroit in 1930, and again in 1932, were overwhelmed by the economic needs of their cities, and concerned about the social and political ramifications of failure to meet those needs. In 1932 the mayors of 29 cities, including New York, Boston, and Chicago, met to discuss their common problems. They were agreed that the need was beyond the means of cities, counties, and states, that it required federal intervention in terms of public works, relief, and loans. Congress was willing but Hoover was not, and very little was done to ease the urban burden in that year.

The mayors who had met in 1932 were mostly Democrats. Republicans shared much of their aggravation, but were not generally willing to draw the conclusion that only a change in administrations in Washington would bring a change in national policy. The mayors did meet again in 1933, with 49 cities then represented. They appealed once more for help, and also created a new organization, the U. S. Conference of Mayors, which would continue to represent their demands.

During the New Deal years, since most major cities had gone Democratic, the mayors and their organization had real power. Moreover, these were people with some political importance, as I have already noted. While they were never satisfied with the amount of WPA aid their cities got, for example, they were also among its staunchest supporters; the mayors not only supported agencies like WPA, but supported federal rather than state direction—city control would be ideal, but barring that, Washington was a good deal more to be trusted than the state capitol.

Moreover, it became increasingly apparent to Roosevelt, as the New Deal years unfolded, that city leaders and city voters were among his strongest supporters, both in terms of what he was trying to do and of simple political support. The city bosses like Kelly of Chicago, Hague of Jersey City, Flynn of the Bronx (who was also a major Roosevelt adviser) were his most uncritical supporters, and among the few who stood by him even in his most ill-considered crusades, such as the effort to purge the party in the 1938 primaries. It was the cities especially, and their mayors, who were most enthusiastic about the third term. Few political relationships have been so mutually productive.

A number of interesting questions arise about the relationship of the New Deal and urban politics. It was a complex and reciprocal set of relationships, really, and they have been studied in depth by very few scholars. For some reason, the New Deal's effects on the states have been of more interest to historians, despite the central importance of cities and city politics in recent history. This is a key reason for the overgeneralization and simplification that have thus far attended the urban dimension of New Deal politics.

One of the main examples of this is the so-called "Last Hurrah" thesis, taking its name from Edwin O'Connor's popular novel and film of that name, based loosely on the career of James Michael Curley of Boston. Briefly, O'Connor's argument was that the New Deal killed the old time political boss because it nationalized and usurped the traditional welfare-type activities that had held the urban poor to the machine. It was an argument that seemed, on the face of it, very logical, and was thus persuasive. It is not entirely invalid, although it can be and has been qualified to the point that it remains at best a partial explanation for the decline of the machine, as we shall see.

But I think both the supporters and the detractors of the "Last Hurrah" thesis have tended to look at too few of the dimensions of urban politics that influenced the New Deal or were affected by it. Things become clearer if we are a bit more comprehensive.

One factor of importance, often underestimated, was the extent to which the New Dealers, including Roosevelt, were real reformers—in the sense of people who put policy considerations ahead of purely partisan ones. This was certainly less true of Jim Farley and Ed Flynn, for example, than of Harry Hopkins and Frances Perkins, and FDR himself was always somewhere in the middle—cognizant of the political realities in which policy had to be molded. Nonetheless, there are incidents where the leaders of the New Deal avoided the politically expedient in favor of advancing their policy considerations. This was quite congruent with Roosevelt's traditional animosity toward Tammany Hall, for example, that led him in the 1930s to throw administration support to an ideologically compatible Republican, Fiorello La Guardia, rather than to Tammany-dominated Democrats.

One good summary of the inadequacies of the "Last Hurrah" thesis can be seen in Pittsburgh. Like other industrial cities Pittsburgh shifted its voter sympathies in the early 1930s: it went Democratic for president in 1932 for the first time since 1856; Democratic party registrations rose from very low in 1929 to a majority in 1936; and a Democratic mayor was elected in 1933, commencing a local Democratic control that continues today. Moreover, the sources of this victory were well understood by the new mayor, William McNair: "They were voting for Roosevelt—they didn't care anything about me."

Thus a party that was used to being on the outs suddenly found itself with voter support, statewide party strength under Joe Guffey, and a supportive national administration with programs that created unprecedentedly great patronage. In this city, at least, it was more a case of the New Deal building a political machine than of it destroying one. Guffey was one of the most successful state Democratic leaders, and he did get thousands of jobs for the state; moreover he directed their distribution in a partisan fashion. Pittsburgh deserved recompense for its strong Democratic vote. And if Governor Pinchot, a Republican, complained that the WPA "had been sold into political bondage," the state's WPA administrator responded that "the Republicans would do the same thing if they had WPA, wouldn't they?" Of course.

The fact was that almost all New Deal programs were tempered by American federalism and state fears of national dictation. This resulted in endless possibilities for local intervention and manipulation—good or evil—of the programs. WPA projects, for example, were initiated by state and local government. They were then reviewed by district offices, and ultimately approved in Washington; then the state administrator would choose from among those nationally approved. Thus, the WPA administrative bureaucracy was itself huge and, as appointive, primarily Democratic. There were both organizational and partisan avenues for local intercession. The welfare program set up by the early relief legislation also went through local government; it was the cities and counties that distributed the jobs and the money, no matter where the resources came from. This continued with the Social Security system, basic parts of which were reserved to local government; county welfare administrations therefore had a great deal of largesse to dispense, and they were rarely separate from the local urban machine in populous counties.

Thus, the Pittsburgh Democrats, for example, were able to move people from relief to WPA jobs, and back again, as the need demanded. The people continued to encounter the politicians. And the proportion of party activists who were on the public payroll increased in this decade in Pittsburgh (48% of Democratic precinct committeemen, versus 20% of the Republicans were on the public payroll in 1940), again suggesting the nonseparation of politics and welfare.

The same situation occurred in other cities. Had New Deal relief and welfare legislation created an entirely federal welfare system, the effects on urban political machines might have been considerable. But such legislation could never have been passed, and wasn't even tried.

This was only part of the problem. The New Deal did weaken the machine indirectly because it removed increasing parts of the urban population from reliance on the kind of welfare services the machine did best. This is clearest in the long term with the rise of organized labor. As poverty declined, so too did the traditional base of machine operations. Thus, for those urban people who moved into a new economic position, it was necessary for the urban Democratic machine to change, to become more issue-oriented and more culturally supportive. It was reliant on the national administration for many things. The money of course came from there, but so did a good part of the popular support, as Mayor McNair noted.

Urban politics had changed to the extent that it was clearly part of a local–state–national continuum, more than before. And it would be much harder than before—increasingly impossible in fact—for a local Democratic boss or organization to exist outside the south without accommodation to a national Democratic administration.

These several forces can be seen in the relationship of the Roosevelt administration to the Pendergast machine of Kansas City. This was an old machine, going back to the late nineteenth century, that, under Tom Pendergast reached its greatest heights in the 1920s and 1930s, but with an unsavory reputation for bossism and corruption. In the 1920s the machine had become an important county as well as city force, and when the state turned Democratic in the 1930s, Pendergast's importance was even further enhanced.

The Pendergast machine responded to the exigencies of the Depression with an ongoing organization and traditional sources of funds—meaning that Kansas City fared probably better than less machine-dominated cities during the Hoover years. Moreover, Pendergast was an early supporter of Roosevelt's bid for the presidency, and Missouri and Kansas City consequently benefited in the early distribution of relief funds. Later in the decade, the WPA was also politically controlled; it strengthened the machine, but also provided employment for thousands of Kansas City families.

Thus, in the short run the New Deal did not really hurt the Pendergast machine, despite the unhappiness of many New Dealers in cooperating with it. Through local administration and distribution of welfare, New Deal programs were a key source of machine patronage, and thus of the machine's strength.

On the other hand the New Deal did provide at least implicit controls on Pendergast's actions. He had to play the game within New Deal defined boundaries; he had to anticipate just what Roosevelt would let him get away with, just how far he could politicize New Deal programs, without bringing down the not inconsiderable wrath of the administration.

The Pendergast machine did fall by the end of the 1930s, although the reasons were complex. Federal forces were involved at the outset, in the form of the federal district attorney in Kansas City, who began an election fraud investigation. This emboldened Pendergast's local rivals, especially the governor, Lloyd Stark. The governor was an important competitor because he had his own sources of patronage from state-directed federal programs. He also had enough clout in this case to argue strongly to Hopkins and Roosevelt that Pendergast should be overthrown.

But Roosevelt was diffident, letting others try to bring the boss down first. Only after the Pendergast organization was beaten in the 1938 primary, by a combination of the federal attorney, Governor Stark, and the machine's own internal problems, did the president begin to take an active hand—he started to deal with Stark, reappointed the district attorney, and supported a major federal investigation. Pendergast went to prison for income tax evasion and the machine was broken. Thus Roosevelt and the New Deal played a role in overriding this boss and this machine, but only after other forces had made it quite clear that the effort would be successful. Until that time, Roosevelt continued to direct patronage to Pendergast, in effect supporting him.

Roosevelt and New Deal reformers like Hopkins had never liked Pendergast, never wanted to perpetuate what they saw as one of the nation's most corrupt and self-serving urban political organizations. But they also recognized their own need for such organizations' support, and so in this case did not initiate the machine's demise. This is a good example of the reciprocity of federal–city relationships in the Democratic politics of the time, and of the weakness of any one-dimensional explanatory model, whether it be the "Last Hurrah" thesis or its opposite.

In Boston, Roosevelt had never much liked James Michael Curley, who was mayor at the time FDR was running for the presidency. He felt much greater ideological and personal affinity for people like Senator David Walsh, leader of the state organization. But Walsh and most other Massachusetts Democrats were Smith supporters in 1932; Curley was needed then and could not be entirely ignored afterwards. In this case, however, FDR was able to work both ends against the middle, gaining the post-convention support of the Walsh group without alienating Curley entirely. It was often easier to appeal to both city and upstate voters than city and upstate politicians—and Massachusetts was only one example, as chapter 5 will illustrate.

With Boss Frank Hague of Jersey City, the situation was somewhat different. Hague had been pro-Smith into the 1932 convention. But he then offered Roosevelt his support and told him that if he came to Jersey City, Hague would provide "the largest political rally ever held."

He had to make amends with the impending national administration for his organization's well-being. And Roosevelt needed New Jersey, which he was much more likely to get if he had the support of the strong if unsavory Hague.

Hudson County (Jersey City) did vote 71 percent for Roosevelt in 1932, and 78 percent in 1936; it also voted over 70 percent Democratic in the congressional elections of the decade, and was doing so in a state whose party balance was quite close. It was this, plus the fact of the machine's corruption and Hague's personal illiberalism, violation of civil liberties, war with the CIO, and so on, that created another political conundrum the New Deal could only try to live with. The New Dealers did give him patronage, five million dollars for his spectacular medical center, Roosevelt's presence to dedicate the center in 1936, and other support. At the same time it tried to stay at arm's length from him, to project an image of not approving or supporting him, which was hardly easy. Unfortunately, no viable local source of opposition arose in New Jersey the way it did in Missouri, and so the New Deal ended up supporting the Hague machine throughout, as the cost of its own survival.

A more agreeable merging of the ideological and political can be seen in Charleston, S.C. Here, the city Democracy was divided between an old stock, aristocratic group, and a more reformist and democratic one led by an Irish Catholic. They fought bitterly in the primaries, which were the only elections that counted in South Carolina, and business leaders led in a compromise mayoralty in 1931, where both sides supported the choice of Burnett Maybank.

Maybank did not hold together the two traditional Democratic factions for long, but he was nonetheless successful in the 1930s. Charleston was in a very bad economic shape during the Depression, and was not financially able to deal with its own relief needs. Maybank provided the national orientation the city needed. He was a strong supporter of the New Deal and Roosevelt, and was also friendly with Senator James F. Byrnes and Harry Hopkins as well. He was the kind of modern, cautious reformist that New Dealers were looking for, and Charleston did very well in terms of New Deal relief funds. This enabled Maybank to build his own organization, apart from the traditional factions. He shortly became a regional political power, the effective head of the county Democracy, and was easily reelected in 1935, moving on successfully to the governorship in 1939.

This was a case of ideological as well as political reciprocity between a city administration and the New Deal, and such cases were by no means rare, although they were much more likely to exist outside the great metropolitan centers.

It is important to interpose here a caution of sorts that we not get so bogged down in the partisan aspects of the federal–local relations that we forget the policy factors. New Deal programs did produce real change in the cities, not only in terms of short-run dealing with relief needs but in a number of long-term areas as well. Relief projects built schools and hospitals and parks and roads, accumulated information of various kinds, and provided culture for the masses—all with effects well beyond the simple giving of jobs to the indigent. Moreover, New Deal programs also created a new and permanent relationship, as in public housing, wherein the cities could anticipate continuing federal aid to deal with the housing, health, and other needs of their people.

This had the effect of making city politicians somewhat more optimistic and ambitious about what they could hope to do to solve their social problems. It also tended to separate the cities from their states, from where most of their economic support had previously come. City governments were more powerful because they now had a way to get around the state legislatures, which had always seemed impecunious and rural. The focus of government was becoming more federal and urban, with the states losing out. The cities were increasingly reliant on the federal government—indeed, they needed it to survive once these programs had begun—but they had a new independence at the same time.

This, too, was not without its purely political considerations, and here also reciprocity played a role. Roosevelt learned the big city mayors were important political allies. When, for example, he wanted to defeat the Ludlow resolution, which would require a national referendum before a declaration of war, he told Farley to "call up Hague and Kelly and get their delegations lined up." Farley did so, and Hague and Kelly talked to the Jersey City and Chicago congressional delegations who contributed to the 209–188 vote against bringing the measure to the House floor. Similarly, in the midst of his campaign to get Alben Barkley elected senate majority leader, FDR asked Farley and Hopkins to tell Mayor Kelly to put pressure on Illinois Senator William Dietrich; Dietrich switched to Barkley. And the president turned again to Hague, to get his support of moving the Assistant Secretary of the Navy to the New Jersey governorship to facilitate his appointment of another man as new Secretary of the Navy.

Everything was political, in one way or another, in the complex set of interrelationships between the New Deal and the cities. But their effects influenced far more than politics. The nature and considerations of urban government were changed, as we have seen; and, in response, the nature and committed obligations of national government were altered as well.

The relationship between the New Deal and the two largest cities provides examples of the operation of most of the ideas thus far offered in this chapter, and will round out our inquiry into the various ways in which urban politics changed as a result of the Roosevelt years in Washington.

In New York, Tammany Hall was the Democratic organization of Manhattan, one of the city's five boroughs (each of which comprised also a separate county). But it had always been the most important of the five city machines, and often had real control over the others, as in the days of Boss Charles Francis Murphy (1902-1924). Tammany, indeed, was in its heyday in the Murphy years, winning a lot of elections, influencing politics throughout the city, and even the state, and contributing some good government in the process. Even then, however, there were Democrats as well as Republicans who continued to oppose it. For every Al Smith and Robert F. Wagner who rose to political respectability through Tammany, there was an upstate or silk-stocking Democrat like Franklin Roosevelt who saw the machine as inherently evil. Tammany was a bad word in many places, partially for the evils it may or may not have been committing, partially for the groups it represented, partially for its past.

With Murphy's death Tammany fell on hard times. It failed to generate a strong leader. And the quality of its candidates fell off with the mayoralty of Tammanyite James J. Walker (1925-1932). "Jimmy" Walker's optimism and superficiality, his night-clubbing and glad-handing did represent an image that some New Yorkers idealized—but this was hardly true for the masses. His conduct did little for the efficacy of government per se, and by the time of the Depression it began to wear, at the very least. Tammany could not control Walker, nor the state investigation into his mayoralty that began during his second administration. And when it looked like Governor Roosevelt might have to remove him, Walker resigned, weakening Tammany as well as his own image in the process.

In 1932 the time seemed propitious for either anti-Tammany

Democrats or Fusion (with the Republicans as weak as they were in New York City, their only chances for victory tended to be in terms of fusing with other alienated groups). In the special mayoral election of 1932 the Tammany man, Surrogate (judge) John P. O'Brien did win, but narrowly; the acting mayor, Joseph V. McKee, an anti-Tammany Democrat, received over a quarter million write-in votes. Thus, the perpetuation for the very short term—until the regular mayoral election of 1933—of Tammany control did not signify any lessening of anti-Tammany strength both within and without the party.

McKee was from the Bronx, an Ed Flynn man rather than a Tammany one. Roosevelt asked Flynn to persuade McKee to run for the full term in 1933; it seemed the only way to keep New York Democratic. And the Republicans, for their part, had seen again in the 1932 special election how weak they were by themselves; the pro-Fusion elements in the party had a convincing argument once again. But Fusion meant La Guardia in 1933, since he had told the Republican leaders that if he didn't get his party's nomination he would run anyway, which meant sure defeat for any other anti-Tammany candidate.

Thus, in 1933 New York City had an interesting three-man mayoral race. Mayor O'Brien ran again, representing Tammany. McKee finally succumbed to the urging President Roosevelt, Flynn, and Farley to run on a third ticket: the Recovery Party. And La Guardia ran on the Fusion ticket, winning the election with 42 percent of the vote to 30 percent for McKee and 28 percent for O'Brien. Tammany was in disarray, the New Deal had suffered a partisan defeat, and an independent, sort-of-Republican/sort-of-New Dealer was in power in the city.

Fiorello H. La Guardia was one of the more interesting figures to emerge in American politics in the 1920s. Of a multi-ethnic, middle class background, widely travelled, with a strong sense of identity with the urban masses and an ability to talk with them (he spoke the languages of New York's Jews, Italians, Puerto Ricans, and others), he had excellent credentials for success in New York politics. He was a Republican, however, which was a disadvantage. He had made that decision, like some other idealistic young New Yorkers, out of repugnance for Tammany, but it put him into a party that shared neither most of his ideas nor the same kinds of supporters as would provide the eventual base of La Guardia's power.

His Republicanism did not impede his election to Congress from the lower east side in 1916, and again in 1918, nor did it stop his moving up to President of the Board of Aldermen in 1919 after a distinguished career as a flyer in World War I. La Guardia then ran in the 1921 Republican mayoral primary, losing to the machine candidate. The next year he began a ten-year second career in Congress, representing upper Manhattan. He became well known in Congress as a liberal, opposing Prohibition, supporting labor (the Norris-La Guardia Anti-Injunction Law), public power and unemployment insurance, and so on. He did fail as a Republican candidate for mayor in 1925, losing to Jimmy Walker by a half-million votes; but the scandals of the second Walker administration sent La Guardia to Gracie Mansion in January 1934, where he stayed for three four-year terms.

La Guardia shared most of the ideas of the New Dealers, despite his party difference; he was also a great supporter of Roosevelt and his programs. And he benefited as well from the administration's largesse. It was clumsy, certainly unfortunate, but nonetheless inevitable—the nation's largest city had a mayor who was extremely supportive of New Deal aims, and was entirely cooperative, but was also a Republican. The answer had to be cooperation, even if Jim Farley and Ed Flynn did a lot of teeth gritting in the process. New York City received as grants or loans about one-quarter billion dollars from PWA programs; it got about $150 million per year from WPA, and the moneys were used reasonably well.

La Guardia always accused Tammany of playing politics with relief, and some people accused him of the same. But in fact he did much less of this than most, partially because of his idealism, but also because he may have had a personal organization yet never really fit into a party one. He always openly supported Roosevelt for president, for example, and worked actively for him in New York. In turn, Roosevelt supported La Guardia, despite their party differences, and never permitted relief funds to be used in a way to undercut the mayor.

La Guardia had always used Tammany and the boss system, in Ed Flynn's words, as "whipping boys"—it was one of the few avenues a nonDemocrat had to gain office in New York City. But in the 1930s he was not the only one putting pressure on Tammany Hall. Flynn and Farley, representing the president, were also commited to bringing the New York Democracy out of Tammany control. They strived to put their own men in charge of the other boroughs' party organizations—Flynn himself in the Bronx, Frank Kelly in Brooklyn. Tammany patronage from Washington was cut, and in 1934 for the first time in history a Tammany Hall leader—John Curry—was deposed.

The Tammany leaders of the Manhattan Democracy were rather

out of touch with things. They continued to be overwhelmingly Irish, unrepresentative of other Manhattan groups, especially in Jews and Italians. They were politically reactionary, fighting Roosevelt, the New Deal, Governor Herbert Lehman—and ignoring the valuable lesson of Charlie Murphy, that the successful leader has to accept modernization and the people's will to stay on top. Thus, Tammany lost control of city hall for twelve long years, even though the Democrats were doing well at other levels in city voting.

Table 4.4 gives the vote for the five boroughs of New York City during the 1930s. It shows clearly enough that La Guardia's rise to local power did not mean a decline of Democratic popularity in New York City. Majorities for president and Congress continued very high in all the boroughs, including Manhattan, and were in fact the key element in state-wide Democratic fortunes as well. It was the extent to which the Democrats swept the city that often decided the outcome of New York state elections.

In the process, however, local politics was obviously affected. Even to the Democrats the price of overcoming Tammany was a large one. Not only did a nonDemocrat hold city hall for twelve years, but, beyond that, the New York Democracy, and especially that of Manhattan, was permanently divided. By 1936 the American Labor Party was functioning in Manhattan; it was a combination of liberal and labor (especially the Jewish garment trades) groups, anti-Tammany and pro-New Deal, working to ensure Roosevelt's reelection outside the party system (it gave him a quarter-million votes in 1936). It became important in New York local politics. Because of its Italian and Jewish, intellectual and working class combinations of support, it had the potential for balance of power strength.

This can be seen in the successful New Deal effort to purge Congressman John O'Connor in 1938. O'Connor was chairman of the House Rules Committee, a long-time Tammany loyalist with no affinity for New Deal legislative programs over which his position gave him considerable control. He was also out of touch with his district, whose demography had undergone drastic changes during his time in the House. And he had paid no attention to the rising opposition to Tammany of the New Deal years. His opponent in the Democratic primary, James Fay, was supported by La Guardia as well as Roosevelt and ran as a committed New Dealer. Tammany supported O'Connor. Thus, the contest was a combination of local and national factors, with Fay successful. But O'Connor then turned around and won the Republican

TABLE 4.4

Vote of the Five Boroughs of New York City[a]

(Percent Democratic)

	Manhattan	Bronx	Brooklyn	Queens	Richmond
1930 Congress	63	68	60	63	67
1932 President	67	70	67	62	61
1932 Congress	68	71	65	63	66
1934 Congress	62	66	63	66	56
1936 President	68	67	64	62	63
1936 Congress	68	75	71	65	66
1938 Congress	52	53	56	57	59

[a]Vote for New York (Manhattan), Bronx, Kings (Brooklyn), Queens, and Richmond counties. See Appendix for description of statistics, data, and methods.

nomination! He was beaten by Fay in the general election, however, but as a result of the American Labor Party; the Democratic and Republican votes were nearly equal, ALP provided Fay's winning edge.

By the end of the decade things would get more confused, as the liberal and labor groups in the ALP found themselves in combat with the Communists for control, resulting by the mid-1940s in leaders of the former (such as David Dubinsky, Alex Rose, and Luigi Antonini) quitting the American Labor Party to found the Liberal Party—and resulting also in the ALP's decline.

But what is most important is that a new party was formed that in many respects reflected the La Guardia approach to politics: liberal Democrat in national and state affairs, but ideological, pro-reform, anti-machine and boss (especially Tammany) in local matters. It became a permanent element in New York City politics, diminishing thereby the power of the Democrats. Had Tammany been more responsive to the realities of the 1920s and 1930s this would very possibly not have happened. But the individual importance of La Guardia, and the ideological commitment of the New Dealers to support people like him regardless of party, and to oppose Tammany on principle, also played their part in the process. The Democrats, for all their general strength in New York, came out of the New Deal years with a weaker grasp on the city itself than they had possessed before.

Chicago was quite different. The machine did not fail, for several reasons. Chicago was not a divided city like New York; there was much less faction among Chicago Democrats by 1930—Tony Cermak was taking care of that; and the Chicago Democracy found itself able to live with the New Deal ideologically as well as politically.

The New Dealers, on the other hand, had mixed feelings about the Chicago Democratic machine. Politicians like Farley were impressed by the reluctance with which Cermak had come over to the Roosevelt forces and wanted to punish him by withholding patronage, despite the strong Democratic victory in Illinois in 1932. It was in response to this that Cermak went to confer with Roosevelt in February 1933, but met instead with the assassin's bullet that resulted in his death a few weeks later.

These patronage considerations were patched up soon enough, with the new party leaders, Mayor Edward J. Kelly and Patrick A. Nash. More enduring were the attitudes of New Dealers like Ickes—who had spent much of his early career in Chicago—that the machine was little better than Tammany and should be treated similarly. They hoped that the New Deal could reform Chicago politics in some way similar to what they believed was happening in New York at the same time. When Kelly ran for his first full term in 1935, for example, Ickes tried to persuade the president to oppose him; but Farley argued the contrary very forcefully—Kelly would win regardless, and the president would suffer if he fought the inevitable. This kind of reasoning always impressed FDR, and he deferred to it.

There was simply not the divergence between local and national politics in Chicago that there was in New York. The Kelly–Nash machine had enormous local popularity, a strong ethnic and working class coalition (which included even three-quarters of the black vote as early as 1935), and bases of power quite apart from the New Deal. Certainly the Democratic connection was very useful; it permitted the machine to build on national Democratic popularity. And certainly also the money and jobs of New Deal programs were very helpful to the machine. But what Cermak had built, and Kelly (and Kennelly and Daley later) enjoyed, was constructed on such solid foundations that by the middle 1930's there was not only no Republican party in Chicago, there was really no viable Democratic opposition either.

The machine did use relief, taking clear advantage of the local administrative aspects of New Deal programs. So far as most poor Chicagoans were concerned their relief checks or their public employment came to them courtesy of the City of Chicago or Cook County, both of which were administrative agencies of the local Democratic party. When a Chicagoan asked his or her congressman for a WPA or other job, it was not unusual to be told that one needed a note from one's ward committeeman in order to get the job. There was only so much relief available, and the machine felt it was only reasonable that it go to Democrats. Thus, the programs did bolster the strength of the machine; the "Last Hurrah" did not come to machine politics in Chicago.

Kelly knew the importance of New Deal support, not only in patronage but also in image. He told the voters in 1935 that "I'll be sitting in President Roosevelt's office. . . . We will go after all the government money we can get." This had seemed reasonable then; it continued to apply in 1939 and 1943 as well. And the president responded not only with patronage but with other support as well. He even went against his advisers' wishes and supported Kelly–Nash in their unsuccessful effort to unseat popular Governor Henry Horner in 1936.

The urban–federal relationship was clearly reciprocal. Chicago had become for national Democrats one of the most reliable vote-producing centers of the nation—generally able to turn out sufficiently high majorities to carry the whole state for the Democratic party. And the machine had come to see the federal government, in its programs and its prestige, as a main financier and general support of the machine's own control of the city. It may not have been an ideal system, as Chicago reformers like Paul Douglas often charged, but it was a reasonably efficient one, and served the citizens of Chicago relatively well (even to the point of putting critic Douglas into the Senate in 1948). The machine survived, as did the boss; so, too did the Democratic party and the New Deal.

The New Deal and Depression had a variety of effects on urban politics—and were variously affected by urban politics in turn. The cities made up an increasingly important part of the new Democratic strength—this was evident at least as early as Al Smith's run for the presidency in 1928. And it was the New Deal and its programs for the poor, labor, and so on that led to a so-far permanent commitment of the majority of urban citizens to the Democrats.

The federal-city relationship also changed drastically, and permanently in these years. It became much more direct, circumventing the states in many important areas, and it grew much deeper and more meaningful. Henceforth, cities would look to Washington for information, direction, and especially financial support. Whether the urban problem is housing, unemployment, welfare, or any of a great variety of ills, the New Deal years resulted in Washington's replacing state government and private groups, as well as the cities themselves, as the source of potential solutions.

The cities consequently became better equipped to deal with the problems of an industrial and urban population. How good a job they have done in the past forty years is arguable; many would say they have done poorly. But the political system created by the 1930s undoubtedly gave them a better chance to deal with at least the survivalistic problems of their populations than they had previously.

The nature of urban politics also changed. I have argued that the "Last Hurrah" thesis is an oversimplification, and certainly not universally valid. Those machines survived that were able to bend the new realities of a more tightly organized city-state-federal political continuum wherein the people expected more from government than before. Like any institution, the political machine can only survive if it remains timely. Some machines have accordingly done well, although most of them have adopted a style that leads us to call them by other names. Chicago, under the late Mayor Richard J. Daley, is perhaps the major exception of unchanged style; but other changes did take place there, which is why that machine survived. So long as poverty and unassimilation remain there is plenty of room for the type of urban politics practiced by Charlie Murphy and Tony Cermak—focussing on the individual and responding to his or her immediate needs. This has not changed. It has only been made more difficult by the increasing percentages of city dwellers who managed—often via New Deal programs—to move out of that tenuous socioeconomic situation.

The cities, finally, became more important. They had an increasingly large part of the population (at least until the post-Second World War movement to the suburbs). Their voting was better organized by unions and other groups, and thus increased in importance. City pluralities alone won seven states in the 1932 presidential election, six in 1936, and nine in 1940. Even the twelve largest cities alone provided sufficient margin for the Democrats to win in 1940, 1944, and 1948.

Beyond voting, the cities, through national programs, became the foci of social and economic change in America. They were and are the laboratories for experimentation in education, housing, and other areas that sought solutions to old and new problems of the twentieth century. We had become, in all these ways, an urban nation.

FIVE

The New Deal in the States

State politics in America occupy a sometimes confusing position between national and local. The state party does fit into the major organizational structure of the national one; state officials—especially governors and senators—are often key national party figures; and the state is the basic cooperative and administrative agency for many national programs. However, the state party organizations are often decentralized, even dominated in some states by one or more local organizations, and their actual voter control is often minimal, which is one reason why in the northeast national politicians have been traditionally more solicitous of big city leaders than those who operate at the state level. Thus, to understand the effects of the New Deal on state politics it is necessary to look in directions other than those of popular voting behavior.

The states needed the new Democratic national administration, often badly. Many state governments had been influenced by the confidence of the 1920s to the point of engaging in deficit spending. The Depression not only made it unlikely that the deficits would be repaid, it also put heavy pressure on increasing them to deal with welfare problems. Both those states that were willing to go into debt for relief purposes and those that were not found themselves in need of federal aid by 1932, and began arguing more and more forcefully for it. Most governors by the end of 1932 shared the feelings of the masses that Hoover's programs were inadequate. Even federal loan programs provided only a fraction of what was needed; the Reconstruction Finance Corporation seemed demanding, inefficient, and niggardly.

State administrations wanted a responsive national government that would provide the money they needed, at no cost to themselves— at least in the eyes of the voters. But as much as they wanted the money to come from outside the state, they insisted that its control remain local. This was one of the reasons why so many New Deal programs (FERA, NYA, social security, etc.) were mixed federal-state in funding and/or administration. Other reasons for this were questions of constitutionality and popular acceptance, which recognized real problems of federalism but resulted in a far too involved administrative structure, a great deal of waste, and general inefficiency.

One of the major problems the early New Deal had with states was in getting them to appropriate monies for the required matching funds for national programs. Fiscal conservatives in some states lobbied against any more deficits; other interest groups argued that the federal money was going only to some, mainly urban, people and should not be matched by general state funds; still others said that federal political power was becoming too strong and should be fought even at the cost of sacrificing federal funds. But the need and desire for federal monies was just too great, and this, along with some strong New Deal politicking to put popular pressure on state governments, resulted in the ultimate cooperation of almost all states.

The relief programs especially opened all kinds of problems. Some governors tried to shift their whole state relief burden to the federal government, which would make them look very good with their own voters. More common was the turning of relief money into a political slush fund of sorts, used for a combination of its designed purpose and also the building of firmer political organization—accomplishing at the state level what urban politicians were doing locally. Such Democratic governors as Bill Murray of Oklahoma and C. Ben Ross of Idaho, as well as some Republicans, were accused of this by the middle of the 1930s, and with cause—what politician could fail to see the tremendous clout involved in all those dollars and jobs?

Another important area was relative city and state power. It is true that, for reasons of numbers and organization, the cities and their peoples became increasingly important in national politics in the 1930s. However, there continued to be tremendous over-representation of rural and small town areas in the state legislatures. As late as 1960, just before the one man–one vote decisions of the Supreme Court, the ratio of largest to smallest population per state legislator still ranged from 3:1 to 1081:1. In 1930, those living in towns with populations under 25,000 had, nationally, about double the voting strength of those in the large cities. In the larger states the disparity was generally greater: in Massachusetts the small town voter had, in effect, a vote four times as powerful as the Boston voter; in New York the small town advantage was almost six to one. What this means is that those population groups that we have seen as relatively less attracted to the New Deal and the Democrats tended to be more influential at the state level than in national politics. This will be an important intervening variable to remember.

Although state politics involves a good deal more than popular voting, that remained the ultimate denominator, which is why I have included the rather cumbersome Table 5.1. This table gives the Democratic vote for each state in the 1930s for President, United States Senator, Governor, and Congressman (either congressman-at-large or the mean of the total state congressional vote). The vote is given less for concern with specific contests than to seek states with firm partisan alignments shown in consistent voting over time. The vote here is not, as above, the Democratic percentage of the two-party vote, but rather the Democratic percentage of the total vote, which is more useful in determining the extent to which a state has become truly Democratic (for precision, I have italicized those cases where the Democrats had a plurality but not a majority of the vote).

It is more meaningful to look at state politics in a regional context, and to relate the materials of Table 5.1 to other aspects of state political effects of the New Deal.

Starting with the northeast, Roosevelt's own state of New York is a good example of a Democratic organization benefiting from national developments to maintain Democratic hegemony. Like many of the industrial states, New York had traditionally witnessed division and contest between New York City and the more conservative, rural, and Republican upstate, with neither establishing itself as clearly dominant statewide. Roosevelt's predecessors, especially Al Smith, had played some role in expanding the Democrats' statewide position. And Roosevelt himself, in his two terms as governor (1929–1933), had established

TABLE 5.1

Statewide Democratic Vote for President, Congress, Senate, and Governor, 1930–1938[a]

(Percentage Democratic)

	Conn.	Maine	Mass.	N.H.	R.I.	Vt.	Del.	N.J.	N.Y.	Pa.	Ill.	Ind.	Mich.	Ohio	Wis.	Iowa
1930:																
Congress	49	39	46	42	48	33	44	43	54	28	54	53	23	52	b	39
Senate	—	39	54	42	49	—	45	39	—	—	64	—	21	—	—	43
Governor	50	45	50	42	49	29	—	—	56	31	—	—	42	53	b	34
1932:																
President	47	43	51	49	55	41	48	50	54	45	55	55	52	50	64	58
Congress	48	50	48	49	55	36	46	48	54	44	53	55	49	52	48	53
Senate	48	—	—	50	—	45	—	—	56	43	52	56	—	52	57	55
Governor	49	50	53	45	55	37	45	—	57	—	58	55	55	53	52	53
1934:																
Congress	54	51	50	50	57	42	46	51	54	50	57	52	49	54	b	52
Senate	52	50	59	—	57	48	46	58	55	51	—	51	47	60	b	—
Governor	47	54	50	49	57	42	—	49	58	50	—	—	46	51	b	54

1936:																
President	55	42	51	50	53	43	55	60	54	57	58	57	56	58	64	54
Congress	54	40	46	48	49	42	52	53	58	55	55	56	52	58	b	49
Senate	—	49	41	48	49	—	53	55	—	—	56	—	53	—	—	50
Governor	55	42	48	43	54	39	52	—	53	—	53	55	51	52	b	49
1938:																
Congress	53	42	46	44	46	40	43	47	54	46	52	49	46	49	b	44
Senate	40	—	—	46	—	34	—	—	54	44	51	50	—	46	b	50
Governor	36	47	45	43	42	33	—	—	50	46	—	—	47	48	b	46

TABLE 5.1 (cont'd.)

Statewide Democratic Vote for President, Congress, Senate, and Governor, 1930–1938[a]

(Percentage Democratic)

	Kansas	Minn.	Mo.	Neb.	N. D.	S. D.	Alabama	Ark.	Florida	Georgia	La.	Miss.	N. C.	S. C.	Texas	Va.
1930:																
Congress	43	b	63	52	b	32	84	99	88	96	98	99	63	99	95	70
Senate	39	36	—	40	—	52	60	99	—	99	99	99	61	99	87	77
Governor	35	b	—	51	b	46	62	81	—	—	—	—	—	99	80	—
1932:																
President	54	60	64	63	70	64	85	86	75	92	93	96	70	98	88	68
Congress	50	b	62	54	b	54	90	98	75	95	99	99	70	98	92	81
Senate	47	—	63	—	b	45	86	89	99	93	99	—	68	98	—	—
Governor	34	b	60	52	b	56	—	90	67	99	99	—	70	—	62	—
1934:																
Congress	49	b	60	52	b	57	90	92	99	99	99	99	65	99	99	73
Senate	—	b	60	55	b	—	—	—	99	—	—	99	—	—	97	76
Governor	46	b	—	51	53	59	87	89	—	99	—	—	—	99	96	—

1936:																
President	54	62	61	57	60	54	86	82	76	87	89	97	73	99	87	70
Congress	47	b	60	51	b	50	94	92	82	94	99	99	71	99	93	73
Senate	48	b	—	b	—	49	87	82	—	99	99	99	71	99	93	92
Governor	52	b	57	56	b	48	—	85	81	99	99	—	67	—	93	—
1938:																
Congress	41	b	59	46	b	44	92	99	96	99	99	99	65	99	99	77
Senate	50	—	61	—	b	48	—	90	82	95	99	—	64	99	—	—
Governor	45	b	—	44	52	46	87	86	—	95	—	—	—	99	97	—

TABLE 5.1 (cont'd.)

Statewide Democratic Vote for President, Congress, Senate, and Governor, 1930–1938[a]

(Percentage Democratic)

	Ky.	Md.	Okla.	Tenn.	W. Va.	Arizona	Colo.	Idaho	Montana	Nevada	N. Mex.	Utah	Wyoming	Calif.	Oregon	Wash.
1930:																
Congress	59	59	62	64	50	99	46	36	50	46	56	41	35	14	47	26
Senate	52	—	52	71	62	—	56	28	60	—	59	—	41	—	29	—
Governor	—	56	59	64	—	52	60	56	—	47	53	—	49	24	25	—
1932:																
President	59	62	73	66	54	67	55	59	59	69	62	56	56	58	58	57
Congress	59	68	73	64	53	71	55	55	55	61	63	54	48	51	47	59
Senate	59	66	66	—	—	67	52	56	—	52	—	57	—	43	39	61
Governor	—	—	—	59	54	63	57	62	49	—	55	56	—	—	—	57
1934:																
Congress	54	59	67	71	50	69	60	60	69	71	52	63	58	55	41	66
Senate	—	56	—	63	55	72	—	—	70	65	49	53	57	b	—	61
Governor	—	48	58	62	—	60	58	55	—	54	52	—	58	b	57	—

1936:

President	58	62	67	69	61	70	60	63	69	73	63	69	61	67	64	66
Congress	59	59	71	72	60	78	62	65	64	58	63	69	57	59	*47*	66
Senate	59	–	68	76	59	–	63	37	55	–	62	–	54	–	49	–
Governor	–	–	–	80	59	71	55	57	51	–	57	51	–	–	–	69

1938:

Congress	59	60	69	64	55	80	59	54	50	66	58	61	47	57	41	61
Senate	62	68	65	–	–	77	58	55	–	59	–	56	–	b	45	63
Governor	–	55	70	72	–	69	44	42	–	62	52	–	40	52	43	–

aSee Appendix for description of statistics, data, and methods. "Congress' vote is either vote for congressman-at-large, or vote of all state congressional districts combined. Congressional and presidential vote from E. Cox, *State and National Voting* (Camden, Conn., 1972). Italics signify Democratic pluralities.

bPresence of powerful third party makes Democratic percentage misleading.

increased personal and party popularity through the institution, after 1930, of probably the first "state New Deal" administration.

On the other hand, both New York and Massachusetts are examples of a situation where success exacerbated intra-Democratic conflict within the major cities and between those cities and their rural and small town hinterlands. Tammany and anti-Tammany in New York City, pro-Curley and anti-Curley in Boston, accompanied in both states by the more ethnic, pro-labor, pro-New Deal urban elements vying with the more old stock rural ones—all were measures of the problems of national Democratic popularity and success. The appeal to all sides of hundreds of thousands of federally funded jobs for patronage, and of the mantle of administration support, created constant tension. The Roosevelt administration could not easily step its way through this morass, and the party's overall success was somewhat tempered, as Table 5.1 suggests, in the second half of the decade.

The case of Pennsylvania was quite different. It was a strongly Republican state, having been carried by only one nonRepublican candidate (Theodore Roosevelt in 1912) and no Democrat in the twentieth century. The William S. Vare machine in Philadelphia, among the most criticized in the country, was also among the tightest and most efficient, to the point that it was able to carry Philadelphia (and thus the state) for Hoover in 1932.

Moreover, there was a New Dealish faction in the Republican party, led by Governor Gifford Pinchot (1923–1927, 1931–1935). Pinchot had been involved in progressive Republican politics since the days of Theodore Roosevelt, and remained popular, extremely ambitious, and perhaps also a bit self-righteous. His 1930 reelection had been over Vare's opposition, so he was as relatively independent of the state Republican organization as he had always been of the national one. He opposed the nomination of Hoover, and did not actively support him once nominated. He also gave quiet support to the 1932 Democratic candidate for senator. His nonpartisanship reflected his own desire to win a Senate seat in 1934; this, plus his understanding of the direction of popular sentiment, led him to criticize his own party and push a rather ambitious legislative program.

Pennsylvania Democrats like party leader Joseph Guffey put constant pressure on Washington to place partisan loyalties above ideology, and to make sure that patronage and vocal support came to them and not Pinchot. And Pinchot, for his part, grossly overestimated the dual loyalty he felt he deserved from Republicans for partisan reasons and

Democrats for policy ones—it was a not uncommon failing of former Progressives. His legislative program did not succeed, and he lost his bid for the Republican senatorial nomination in 1934, a year when the Democrats—campaigning on a "Franklin Roosevelt hasn't failed you, don't you fail him" theme—finally swept the state.

Urban and industrial Pennsylvania would remain in the New Deal coalition, but its rural and small town areas began to drift away by the end of the decade, leaving the state's politics permanently changed but less confidently Democratic than elsewhere. And the more rural areas of the rest of the northeast, sometimes whole states like Vermont and Maine, had neither the ethnic, class, nor intellectual characteristics of urban areas, and showed relatively little response to the political forces of the decade.

Further to the west, Michigan also had a Republican political tradition. Since the beginnings of the Republican party in the 1850s, it had always carried the state for the presidency through 1928, and had failed to carry it for governor only four times; every state legislature but one had been Republican-controlled since the time of Lincoln. And this Republicanism was as firm as ever in the 1920s.

But by 1930 the Republicans were already embattled not only by the Depression, but also by the Prohibition issue, which worked to the Democrats' advantage in Michigan as in other industrial states. The Democrats made their first gains in the cities, especially with Frank Murphy's victory as mayor of Detroit in the fall of 1930. The Republicans still controlled the state that year, but by 1932 it had turned around, and Michigan was a two-party state for good.

Moreover, the Democratization of Michigan existed not only in voting but also in policy. With the accession of Murphy to the governorship in 1937, the Michigan legislature embarked on an ambitious legislative program (liberalized unemployment compensation, old age assistance, etc.; increased money for education and other programs; a civil service law). Murphy's support for the sit-down strikers in the auto industry during his administration was a key element in their success, and, nationally, a symbol of the coming of age of industrial unionism. It also helped cement the relationship between organized labor and the Democratic party in Michigan. In the short run, however, it alienated some Democrats, divided the party, and led to Murphy's loss in his reelection campaign in 1939.

Similar developments took place in Illinois, where the dominant feature was the great Chicago Democratic machine under Anton Cermak and his successors. Roosevelt was so impressed with the political importance of the Chicago Democratic organization that he supported its unsuccessful effort to unseat the pro-New Deal but independent Democratic governor, Henry Horner. And in Missouri he was equally reluctant to confront the corrupt Pendergast machine because it, too, delivered the votes. Pendergast's ultimate downfall came at hands other than those of the national administration.

There were in fact a variety of opinions among New Dealers about how state party organizations should be influenced, from those who sought only political success to those who wanted ideological and policy change. Ultimately a consensus of sorts was worked out, as it had to be, that useful state organizations would be supported regardless of their policies, while at the same time an effort would be made to promote legislation with a New Deal character, general political reform, and social welfare. This realistic approach did not please administration ideologues, but politically it was the only reasonable alternative. Indeed, when Roosevelt deviated from this path, most notably in the 1938 primaries (see next chapter), he and the New Deal suffered their greatest intra-party defeats.

In the south these questions took a somewhat different form. There was no doubt that the south—both deep and border—was secure for the Democrats. Rather, what New Dealers in Washington and their supporters in these states hoped for was that conservative southern politicians could be convinced to support national New Deal programs and to emulate them at the state level. It was recognized at the outset that this would be difficult, since southern conservatism was not only social and racial but economic as well—making some New Deal objectives potentially dangerous in the eyes of southern leaders. Roosevelt did try to implement New Deal programs and policies differently in the south, respecting as much as he could traditional mores. But this was not easy to do, since the programs themselves questioned segregation, class relationships, state rights, institutionalized rural and industrial poverty, and so on. Moreover, to some New Deal administrators these programs and federal monies going to the states were tools for undermining unpalatable southern practices, and they were not anxious to make such compromises.

Thus, the New Deal had a mixed fate in the south, and in the end was much resented, despite the region's continued overwhelming Democratic voting majorities. The Jackson, Mississippi, *Daily News* expressed the general attitude of wealth and power in the deep south during the 1930s. It welcomed the return of the Democrats to national control in 1933, and even supported much of the anti-Depression legislation of that year: public works were good, even public power, and Roosevelt was an admirable leader. On the other hand, the paper was always concerned about "the dole," the undermining of traditional values of individual responsibility, labor unions, the blacks, and increased national power. By 1934 and 1935 the *Daily News* felt that federal policies and big deficits were dangerous: unemployment insurance, for example, "emanated from the minds of a lot of lousy loafers who don't want to work." TVA and the Wagner Act showed the need to "get the federal government out of business." The paper did support the president personally in 1936, but with the threat of an anti-lynching bill and the Fair Labor Standards Act it was sure by 1937–1938 that Roosevelt was "over-ambitious" and that the whole idea of government activism had been a mistake.

Individual states also illustrate this general tendency, as well as some more specific ways in which the New Deal influenced politics in southern states. In Georgia, for example, the New Dealers tried to build on Roosevelt's popularity to promote the success of politicians more amenable to national programs. Eugene Talmadge had been elected governor in 1932 as a fairly typical conservative southerner, leery of federal economic action for both political and economic reasons. As an astute politician, however, once New Deal programs were instituted, he fought to see that Georgia—and thus his own organization—got its share of the dollars and jobs that were being handed out. He struggled with Harry Hopkins over the administration of relief, insisting on local control.

Talmadge also saw clearly enough Roosevelt's popularity, and ran for reelection in 1934 as a "Roosevelt man." But he wasn't, really— neither personally nor in terms of policy. In fact he was increasingly alienated by what was going on in Washington—minimum wages, the rise of organized labor, the wasting of tax dollars to pay high wages to southern blacks, and so on. It was the racial and social threats of the New Deal that bothered Talmadge and other southern conservatives the most. And by the time he entered the 1936 senatorial primary, it was as an acknowledged foe of the New Deal and President Roosevelt. Not surprisingly, the administration supported his opponent, Richard Russell, the incumbent. Despite Talmadge's very real mass base of support in

Georgia, the incumbency and the New Deal image gave Russell a decisive sixty percent victory in the primary election.

At the same time, E. D. Rivers was elected governor on a pro-New Deal platform, promising an end to austerity and the institution of more positive state government as well. Although a "little New Deal" in Georgia was hardly the same as one in New York or Michigan, Rivers' legislative program nonetheless produced better school funding, free school textbooks, increased funds for social services, and better cooperation with federal programs. This little New Deal was short-lived, and by 1938–1940 Georgia retreated to provincialism and Talmadge once again, but its experience nonetheless showed that no state was immune to the political forces of the time, and some of their effects were permanent.

Other southern states followed variations on the same theme. Neopopulist Theodore Bilbo in Mississippi seemed both politically too independent and radical, and socially and culturally too reactionary, for New Deal tastes. The New Dealers could undercut his organization, as in the election of Pat Harrison to the Senate in 1936; but they never entirely overwhelmed him or his popular base. Louisiana was yet more difficult, and even the 1935 death of Huey Long did not end the Long machine's independence from all but minimal national administration influence.

There were real New Deal successes in the south, where individuals and coalitions came to power as acknowledged administration supporters. Burnett R. Maybank in South Carolina and David Sholtz in Florida were leading examples. But overall the south went its own way, always electing Democrats, but Democrats committed more to local customs and institutions than to national party organization or programs. Senators Harry F. Byrd and Carter Glass of Virginia, for example, ran their own tight political empire, which cooperated only occasionally with New Deal programs within the state and led the ideological opposition in Washington as well.

In the south, as elsewhere, political leaders did try to take advantage of the patronage opportunities created by New Deal programs, even if the programs themselves were anathema. This often put them up against administrators, for example in the WPA, who were nonpartisan in their commitment to making the programs work; conflict was not uncommon. New Deal leaders, for their part, were not opposed to having such programs work only to the advantage of Democrats, but when it came to trying to balance off one Democratic faction against another, they were in a more difficult position. It was impossible not to offend some state party leaders.

Southern conservative opposition to the New Deal did not lead to party realignment in the south because the whole southern conservative tradition was rooted in the Democracy. It did not even lead to very frequent socioideological battles in the primaries, since the southern party machines were even tighter and less flexible than northern urban ones. There was political concern, however; leaders like Carter Glass of Virginia and Josiah Bailey of North Carolina may have been publicly circumspect, but privately they were very pessimistic about the future of the south in the new Democratic party. The national events discussed in the next chapter exacerbated their pessimism, but they didn't really know what to do about it. So long as the Democratic party continued to be the vehicle of social and racial control approved by the masses, there seemed little possibility of doing much else than going into opposition in their own partisan home.

The New Deal was not without effect in southern states, influencing legislative programs, contributing some new faces and new ideas, and some increased mass—especially black—orientation to national government and politics. But it did not succeed in making southern Democratic parties, like those in other parts of the country, into cooperative parts of a national political organization. Nor was it able to affect the southern social structure, through politics, in a way at all comparable to the situation in the north.

In the agricultural midwest the New Deal's political effects were less than in the east, except for a few states like Wisconsin and Minnesota where the New Deal years saw the culmination of the swing from Republican insurgency through third-party rebellion to Democratic allegiance. Most agricultural states shared the general swing to the Democrats in 1932 and 1934, but soon after moved back to their traditional Republicanism. Likewise, their internal political orders, in terms of the nature and content of state politics as well as party balance, were relatively unchanged.

South Dakota can serve as an example of one key trend in this area: the failure of state Democratic organizations to rise to their opportunity. As Table 5.1 shows, the state did participate in the Democratic resurgence of the early 1930s, but in 1936 and 1938 the Republicans reestablished control. The reasons for this were as much as anything a function of the conservatism of the state's Democratic party. The people of South Dakota may or may not have been interested in a "little New Deal" for their state, but the Democrats never took a chance of finding out; and with no differences offered, why should the voters give up the political habits of a lifetime?

Major battles in South Dakota politics had traditionally been fought out within the Republican party; it was here that agrarian liberalism, such as it was, had existed in the state in the twentieth century. Thus, the Democratic sweep in 1932 was mainly of older, conservative Democrats, like new Governor Tom Berry, who wanted very much to build a viable Democratic organization in the state, but who was legislatively unambitious, fiscally conservative, and generally quite out of touch with the New Deal and its effects elsewhere. The Berry administration put through an inequitable and controversial "gross income tax," and at the same time eliminated popular programs like state hail insurance and the Child Welfare Commission. The governor also called out the National Guard to expel sit-in strikers from a meat packing plant in 1935, and then called it out again to break the strike itself.

While Berry was thus quite out of tune with policy developments in the national Democratic party, he was entirely attuned to the organizational largesse available through New Deal programs. He was the only governor to also be state relief director, which gave him a good deal of patronage and power. The South Dakota Democrats put pressure on Hopkins and Farley to see that federal programs served the strengthening of their newly incumbent party.

But South Dakota's experience suggests that, at least outside the south, one could not have Democratic success without having that state party reflect to at least some degree the policies and spirit of the national administration. Berry's positions had seriously split the state's Democrats, and despite electoral victory in 1934 things did not look very good for 1936. Berry ran for a second term, attacking the state's Democratic senator, William J. Bulow, who was also running again, for being too pro-New Deal. But Roosevelt and Bulow did win—the latter narrowly—and Berry lost, to be replaced by a Republican governor who was more progressive than he. By 1938 the Republicans were firmly back in control, and have tended to remain so. South Dakota's political tradition had been consistent; it had never experienced, for example, the kind of powerful Republican insurgency that was so evident in neighboring North Dakota and Minnesota. Thus, it may well be that a "little New Deal" administration would not have resulted in permanent Democratic gains. But it is even clearer that the kind of Democratic politics that did come to South Dakota, ignoring if not even opposing the spirit of the national party, offered no likelihood of the party's establishment in the state.

In Nebraska the long-term effect was similar, but for a different reason, the continued insurgency of some of the Republicans, which guaranteed that the Republican party would survive the New Deal years reasonably intact. Its leading figure, Senator George W. Norris, did eventually leave the party, to return to the Senate as a pro-New Deal independent in 1936. And Roosevelt supported him that year over the regular Democratic nominee—another indication of the occasional power of ideology in Roosevelt's actions. The political history of the Wisconsin progressives in the 1930s was similar.

This was the case in much of the agricultural midwest, or at least in those states that did not have large industrial cities to provide a floor of Democratic support. The state Democratic parties found it hard to establish themselves. In part it was because of conservative rural populations that, ultimately, were more antagonized than attracted by New Deal agricultural and other policies. But also the conservatism of state Democratic leaders never really provided an opportunity, when they were in power, for the testing of these kinds of policies at the state level. And the New Dealers in Washington, in their urge to get their policies adopted, tended in the midwest to work with the Republican progressives—who ultimately stayed with their party—to the extent that Democrats sometimes had neither the patronage nor the prestige that they had expected.

The mountain states comprised a distinct area, very much influenced by their western traditions, particularly individualism. Politics had traditionally reflected this, being less partisan than interest-group dominated, and generally conservative. The era of the New Deal changed this somewhat, certainly giving the Democrats a greater power base than they had ever had before—but mainly for the short-term only. Also mass power, especially that of unions, was increased, as was some acceptance of governmental activism. But on the whole traditional western values of conservatism and individualism survived the decade; the New Deal was only a passing phenomenon in this area, less influential than for the rest of the country.

In Montana, for example, since the turn of the century politics had been less between Democrats and Republicans than between the "progressives" and the "interests," labels that may be more functionally than literally true. In the 1920s the state had two relatively liberal Democratic senators, Thomas J. Walsh and Burton K. Wheeler, but within Montana things moved slowly, under the watchful eye of Anaconda Copper. Men like Wheeler and Walsh, ambitious and bright, had learned that they were relatively free in Washington politics so long as they hewed to the line within the state and on issues related to Montana's basic economic interests.

But Montana agriculture had not fared well during the 1920s, worsened with drought, and worsened again with the coming of the Depression, which also cut badly into the state's mining and lumber industries. The Democrats sensed the likelihood of victory in 1932, cooperated more than usual, and did sweep the state. Walsh was named Attorney General in Roosevelt's cabinet, but died before he could take office, leaving Wheeler the obvious leader of the party in Montana. And Montana did well vis-à-vis the New Deal: it was second highest in the nation in receipt of relief monies per capita, much AAA funding also came into the state, and its economy seemed to be turning around.

The effects of this were seen in the strong, sometimes overwhelming Democratic victories in the state in 1934 and 1936. As it turned out, however, the coalition was fragile, consisting of real New Deal supporters, Wheeler progressives, organized labor groups, and even a considerable number of Townsend Plan people—all of whom were looking for the moment at the Democratic party, but few of whom had much affinity for one another.

Wheeler was an excellent example of the ultimate rejection of the New Deal by old progressives, for whom it went too far, especially in denying the sacredness of the individual and intensifying problems of class. He slowly broke away from FDR over issues of monetary policy, centralization of power in Washington and in the presidency, and then the Supreme Court packing plan, wherein he was a leader of the Democratic opposition. The administration responded by redirecting patronage and support to the state's other Senator, James F. Murray, and Congressman Jerry O'Connell.

The result by 1937–1938 was a bitterly divided Democratic party. O'Connell made it clear he was planning to oust Wheeler in the 1940 senatorial primary. Wheeler responded by trying to engineer O'Connell's defeat in the 1938 congressional primary; he failed at that level, but then went on to support O'Connell's Republican opponent in the general election, and this maneuver was successful. Thus, the party was completely divided, only half-a-dozen years after its coming to real power in the state.

This split, which did not heal, was ideological and economic, with the older, more rural and conservative Democrats successfully resisting a New Dealer takeover of their party. But in so doing they condemned their party to future minority status in Montana. It was also influenced by the rather traditional values of Montanans, who were, while not unwilling to accept Washington largesse in time of need, on the whole unsympathetic to federal intervention in their lives.

Colorado was similar. It was among the few states that refused to appropriate matching funds for early New Deal relief efforts. Its mid-1930s liberalism was more Townsendite (and thus socially conservative) than it was Rooseveltian. And in Wyoming and Idaho, while the decade did see a new life for the Democrats, it was never to the point of Democratic predominance, nor even unified Democratic aims and action.

New Deal political effect in the mountain states was hardly negligible, and that should be remembered even in regard to the states discussed above. It was even sharper in one additional state, Utah, where it involved to some degree the overthrow of a theocracy. Utah was similar to the rest of the area in its traditional conservatism and general Republicanism. It was, additionally, the seat of the Church of Jesus Christ of Latter Day Saints, the Mormons, and its population was about 63 percent Mormon. Reed Smoot, who had been in the Senate since the early twentieth century, was one of the Twelve Apostles of the church, which was not apolitical.

In 1932 Smoot was decisively beaten by Democrat Elbert D. Thomas, the latter getting his greatest support in the cities and towns, with Mormon voting unity being considerably shattered. Another church defeat followed, when the people voted 60 percent to 40 percent for repeal candidates for the convention to ratify the Twenty-first Amendment; this was presented by its supporters as part of the Roosevelt recovery program, and by its opponents as inimical to Mormon Church desires. Both the Church and the Republican party were hurt by the outcome.

Republican leaders tried to recoup in 1934 by urging a high Mormon official, J. Reuben Clark, to run for the Senate nomination. Clark was willing, but the polls made it clear that Joseph Smith himself would likely lose if he ran as a Republican in Utah that year, and so the President of the Church, Heber J. Grant, wrote to Clark to make him withdraw: "If you were nominated you would be defeated, and it would be one of the most humiliating things to me that could happen to have one of my counselors nominated for the Senate of the United States and left home." The New Dealers were riding high. The Mormon Church made a strong and clear, if generally implicit, stand for Landon in the 1936 presidential race, accusing Roosevelt of lacking religion and respect for the constitution; its major newspaper, the *Deseret News,* was full of such propaganda. But to no avail; Roosevelt took 70 percent of the vote, way above what he had received in 1932, and the Democrats did well generally. Elbert Thomas was comfortably reelected in 1938, running on a clearly pro-New Deal campaign, despite the controversiality of the court-packing plan and the Purge. Once again the church was openly pro-Republican, and once again it was unsuccessful, while the Democrats built a permanent place for themselves in the state's politics.

The mountain states, as part of the rural west, had traditions that were sorely tested by the New Deal. The great economic need created by the Depression was most important in getting people in these states willing to sacrifice principle for immediate need. Beyond this, social factors like increased working class consciousness also facilitated a national orientation and Democratic growth, and even outlived the immediate economic forces. But over the long run these traditional values proved quite resilient with many people. Susceptibility to federal programs, and even to increased state government activism, declined, and things reverted back most of the way to what they had been before. Western states were influenced by the New Deal in a resurrection of the Democrats, and some new strength for political liberalism; but the idea of governmentalism did not take root there to the extent that it did in other parts of the country, and by the end of the 1930s second thoughts about the whole business were common.

The rest of the rural west was pretty much like the mountain states in political response to the New Deal. Most affected was the switch in popular commitment to the Democratic party; least affected were party leaders. Almost everywhere conservative opponents of the New Deal eventually triumphed; the west may have been more Democratic after 1938 than it had been before, but it was not much changed in general political philosophy or attitude toward the role of government in people's lives.

In Oklahoma, for example, the state's two leading Democrats, Governor "Alfalfa Bill" Murray and Senator Thomas P. Gore, represented a southern and western populist tradition (in fact Gore's career went back almost to the Populists) in opposition to the oil companies, and to the rich generally. This kind of rural liberalism was quite different from what the New Deal was about, and both Gore and Murray opposed the administration on almost every count. Oklahoma did not vote matching funds for FERA relief programs; Gore in the Senate consistently voiced his feeling that FDR "was going too far to fast." Texas, under "Ma" and "Pa" Ferguson was similar. The New Deal had its defenders, in politicians like E. W. Marland in Oklahoma, and Sam Rayburn, Maury Maverick, and the young Lyndon Johnson in Texas. And it also had real mass support. But the traditional nature of both states' politics prevailed.

The major exception in western response was the most urban and varied of western states, California. It was undergoing large-scale population growth and urban increase in the period. It had always been pretty much of a one-party state, dominated by the Republicans, and they by a few entrenched interests. In this, as for most states, the New Deal years brought change: as Table 5.1 indicates, even as late as 1930 the Democrats continued to be weak, but by 1932 this had turned around, and from that time forward the state has had two parties.

The real crisis in California Democratic politics came in 1934, when the problem was not right-wing Democrats, as in so much of the country, but left-wing ones. Upton Sinclair, muckraking novelist, erstwhile socialist, and general radical, mounted his successful campaign for the Democratic gubernatorial nomination on a platform well to the left of the New Deal. He wanted state land colonies for the unemployed, state factories also, state financing of human needs with scrip since money was insufficient, and heavy increases in taxes on the wealthy. His program was EPIC, to End Poverty in California.

There was a good deal of concern, and not a small amount of panic, after Sinclair's nomination. Many, probably most state Democratic leaders, were committed to his defeat in the general election. Roosevelt, too, was ultimately persuaded that Sinclair was too far to the left; and national Democratic leaders either openly supported the Republican candidate or, like the president, made their positions clear by pointedly not supporting the Democrat. Sinclair lost, but with 37 percent of the vote in a three-way race; the lack of Democratic organizational and leadership support was certainly crucial.

Roosevelt was, after all, a centrist, and if his major intra-party challenges were from the conservative wing of his party, this did not mean that he was not also concerned about excesses at the other extreme. Whether Sinclair was actually "extreme" is moot; he seemed so to state and national Democratic leaders, and thus was cut off. Something similar happened in 1938, when Roosevelt supported William Gibbs McAdoo for the Senate, who lost in the primary to Sheridan Downey, Sinclair's running mate in 1934. Potential Democratic office holders were losing in California because the New Deal thought them too radical.

Another effect was that a "little New Deal" did not come to California until 1939, with the gubernatorial administration of Culbert L. Olson, who had the support of both wings of the Democratic party. It did come then, and—whatever the good or bad of defeating Sinclair—it was also clear by the end of the decade that the Democrats were indeed an equal force in California politics, which had certainly not been true before 1932.

The influence of the Depression, the New Deal, and Roosevelt on state politics varied from region to region and state to state. But certainly some general observations can be made. As at other political levels, the most important change was the rise of mass popular support for the Democrats, especially in those states where this had been at a low level previously. Even in areas where the end of the decade saw strong Republican renewal—New England, the mountain states—the Democrats were clearly stronger than they had been in 1930.

And this applies as well to party organization and leadership as to voting strength. Given this committed group of voters, plus the perquisites of Democratic power in national office in a time of unprecedented federal spending and job creation, Democratic organizations were built in all states, and rarely entirely eclipsed later on.

The political division of rural and urban areas in the states was aggravated by the New Deal years in many states, with the cultural-social-ideological differences of the two areas becoming increasingly clear. This resulted in governmental division as well, particularly in state senates that proved most resistant to equitable representational schemes. Only in the 1960s, with the Supreme Court's one man–one vote decisions, would this begin to change.

Equally important, states all over the country did engage in little New Deals of one kind or another. There was much variety among them, and some were much less ambitious than others. But state government did become more active and more positive; taxes rose and services along with them. Welfare activities, concern for the economically and otherwise deprived, all increased. Government reorganization was common, sometimes even effective. And bureaucracy increased as well, with all the problems of waste and insensitivity that have become part of the bureaucraticization package.

States lost a good deal of power in these years and after, as first the executive and legislative branches and then the judicial approved a steady extension of federal power at their expense. The traditional police powers, which had guaranteed state control over many aspects of their citizens' lives, were eroded. And the cities became in many respects the key partners of the federal government in policy as well as politics. But it is possible to exaggerate the change; many avenues for state difference and individuality survived the New Deal. The states remained a dynamic and important, if changed and lessened, arena of American political activity.

SIX

The New Deal in National Politics

National political affairs in many respects reflect and are influenced by local and state politics. Thus, the most important national political development of the period was identical to that in the states and cities— the rise of a new majority coalition behind the Democratic party. Likewise the presence of an enormous federal patronage permitted the New Deal considerable leverage in national political affairs, and convinced many senators and congressmen of the advantage of becoming part of the New Deal party system.

Roosevelt in fact had a good deal going for him. The grueling difficulties of the Depression, combined with the strong Democratic victory of 1932 and the president's own ambition, resulted in his receiving unparallelled cooperation and delegations of power from Congress to deal with the crisis. Presidential leadership and especially presidential power reached unprecedented heights. And the size and scope of activities of the federal government were also unprecedented. These are some of the important political changes of the decade, and were also themselves issues with the passage of time.

In the first administration, the presidential-congressional relationship seemed strong and congenial. One study of Congress during the first two Roosevelt years found that, on a group of about 600 votes in the Senate and about 3500 in the House, all but eight percent of the Democratic votes supported the president, and nearly 50 percent of the Republican votes did the same. Throughout the first administration, even including the radical Second Hundred Days of 1935, the executive and legislative branches seemed a real team, under the obvious leadership of the executive branch, and one might well have felt that a new day of active and cooperative politics was underway.

The judiciary did not fit into this lovely picture, however. Dominated by old line conservatives, and immune to patronage, reelection, or other kinds of political pressures, the Supreme Court was a key element in the New Deal equation. Since so much of the political, as well as ideological, heart of the New Deal was based in its legislative program, the position of the Court was crucial. And New Dealers from the start were suspicious of the "nine old men." It took a while for New Deal legislation to work its way up to the highest court, but by 1935 it was becoming increasingly clear that here a real political and ideological stumbling block did exist. First, part of the NIRA was invalidated, then the Railroad Pension Act, then the rest of the NIRA, the Bituminous Coal Act, and a key taxing provision of the Agricultural Adjustment Act. "Little New Deal" measures, such as New York's minimum wage law for women, met the same fate as national legislation. It is true that several of the decisions were unanimous, or nearly so, reflecting some sloppy law-drafting and some truly questionable delegations of congressional authority to the executive. But it is equally true that some of the decisions were clearly ideological, narrowly decided, and entirely out of tune with public desire. The courts were more immune to presidential leadership than Congress; but they were not entirely immune, and Supreme Court conservatism would lead to one of Roosevelt's most divisive political battles.

There were some political problems outside the relationship with the courts in the early years. Even those congressmen voting for New Deal programs were not always enamored of them. In their hesitancy they reflected their constituents on some matters; as early as fall, 1935, one of the first Gallup polls found 60 percent of the population feeling relief and recovery expenditures were "too great"—even 36 percent of the Democrats felt that way. It was in that year that Democratic legislators began to articulate more forcefully their concern, especially over spending and presidential power. Senator Charles McNary (Ore.) wrote at the time that "the president has lost considerable of his influence with his party and has developed a rather childish peevishness." And Senator Key Pittman (Nev.) wrote to FDR that too many Senators were beginning to forget their indebtedness to the president, becoming too self-interested and ambitious, and consequently unreliable.

All of this again points to the increased importance of ideology in the New Deal years. Although some congressional Democrats here and there were critical, this was particularly true of southerners, who saw the New Deal programs, as well as the increased power of the federal government, as moves in the wrong direction. Here ideology also got involved with patronage, as when the president held back on federal appointments in the south until he got commitments on the early emergency relief legislation. "Cotton Ed" Smith of South Carolina soon complained that ". . . if they do not change their method of distributing patronage, the President will soon have a revolution on his hands." And this was in 1933. With the increased radicalization of the legislation of the Second Hundred Days, both the ideological and the patronage aspects of New Deal programs were that much more offensive to southerners like Smith and Walter F. George of Georgia. They, like southern voters generally, were entirely committed to the Democratic party. But they did not like big government, or the rise of labor, or the new disregard for private property—or the liberal and abrasive people in Washington who seemed to control so much, including federal patronage.

There were indeed personal factors in the political dynamics of Washington. Numerous New Dealers, including some of the cabinet officers, did see themselves as above politics and party. They were sometimes insensitive to the real political needs of congressmen and others, expecting them to have the same ideological and administrative orientation as they did. But elected legislators lived in a different world and resented the failure of many New Dealers to try to understand their problems. Moreover, the New Deal attracted many bright, impatient, abrasive young people; they and the more courtly, old-fashioned legislators, especially from the south, would inevitably have personality conflicts. This was a problem that FDR and Farley recognized, but could not really change.

In a way the president himself contributed to it. He was also prone to ideological politics, for all his fabled partisan wisdom. In 1934, for example, he maintained a nonpartisan stance, hoping this would attract nonDemocrats to vote for pro-New Deal candidates regardless of party.

He severely limited the political participation of cabinet members to ensure this nonpartisanship. But its main effect was divisiveness within his own party, which was really more important, since the New Deal was, after all, a Democratic phenomenon. In fact a more partisan stance would have better guaranteed the success of New Deal ideology, but FDR did not see it so at the time. He did change in 1936, making a more partisan campaign, as well as a more left-wing one, since these were clearly the two bases for the overwhelming majority of his support. They were also somewhat conflicting bases, but this became more apparent only after 1936.

Still, at the time of the 1936 election, division was less real than apparent, less a factor than a nuisance. The president won overwhelmingly, and carried record-setting congressional and state-house majorities in his train. The feared coalition of left-wing opposition never really came into being, and the Union Party was a dud. So, too, it seemed at the time, were the Republicans. The Democrats had 75 percent majorities in Congress, obvious public support for what the first administration had done, a president of unprecedented strength and popularity. It seemed that with the possible exception of the courts—and important decisions were expected shortly—Roosevelt and the New Dealers were in firm control of their party, and their party of the nation. This was not in fact true, and an important long-term political rupture was soon to surface.

Roosevelt's decision to do battle with the Supreme Court by enlarging it to bring in more sympathetic members was not entirely surprising, given the disruptive role the court had played by 1937 and the disastrous effect such reasoning would have if continued during the next year, when much of the Second Hundred Days would come before it. But the president's approach was drastic, and his means were disingenuous; he made bad political decisions. The end result was an alienated Congress and an increasingly suspicious public.

The president was not without some popular support at the outset. Even in 1935, in a Gallup poll, 55 percent of the Democrats polled (but only 14 percent of the Republicans) favored some limits on the power of the Supreme Court to declare acts of Congress unconstitutional. And a majority (53 percent) agreed in 1936 that such power should require more than a five-to-four vote. In early 1937, the public seemed to agree (59%) that some change in the court was necessary. But general sympathy for the president and for his frustration with the courts did not translate into support for the court-packing plan itself. Forty-seven percent of the population did express support of the plan in April 1937, but that was not a majority; and the favorable response rate constantly declined thereafter, to about 32 percent by August. The highly publicized battle in Congress moved the people away from the president.

Roosevelt outfoxed himself politically. So far as the public was concerned, he might well have done better with a frontal attack, emphasizing the court's conservatism and its effect on the expressed public will; his stress on the age of the justices and the effect thereof on court efficiency was a palpable falsehood and a tactical mistake. Likewise, this president who had worked so well with Congress really did not consult congressional leaders about the court-packing bill (or the executive reorganization measure that he introduced at about the same time), and this too was a glaring political error. When Roosevelt saw the weak support he was receiving in Congress and from the public generally—almost no labor groups, for example, except for the incipient CIO—he should have withdrawn. But he didn't, and pushed on month after month despite the counterindications. Even the death of his Senate leader, Joe Robinson, did not deter him. Indeed, he put great pressure on his fellow Democrats as often as he could. Robinson himself had persevered in part because of Roosevelt's promise of a Supreme Court seat for himself if successful. Patronage was used, with judicial appointments held up in the states of congressional leaders who were not supportive. Even so committed a New Dealer as Senator Claude D. Pepper of Florida became cautious about presidential power, and resented the fact that in the court-packing battle "opposition to the president may cut off appropriations and patronage."

The effects of all this were considerable. Not only did the plan fail, it ultimately seemed to have been unnecessary, although it may well be that the votes of especially Justice Roberts were not uninfluenced by what had taken place. Nonetheless, divisiveness ensued that was never entirely healed, although that may be largely due to additional factors that emerged in the next year. Not only were the conservatives in the Democratic party alienated from the president, but many of the liberals were also affected and never again quite so sympathetic to Roosevelt, certainly never so subservient to his power. FDR's group of about seventy dependable Senators of January 1937 had been at least temporarily halved by the summer of that year. Ideologically marginal senators moved into the anti-New Deal camp. And the Republicans, few as they were, became more united than they had previously been in the decade.

The latter stages of the court-packing battle had also seen a battle over the Democratic Senate leadership. When Joe Robinson died, Pat Harrison of Mississippi and Alben Barkley of Kentucky were the main candidates. Both had been sympathetic to the New Deal and to Roosevelt personally, but Barkley more so, and he had supported the court-packing bill while Harrison had opposed it. I have shown in an earlier chapter how Roosevelt used his clout with Mayor Kelly of Chicago to get him to persuade Senator Dietrich of Illinois to support Barkley. The president worked at persuading others as well and Barkley won by one vote. But this presidential victory came at a cost; again Roosevelt seemed to be unduly interfering with congressional business, and too partial and ideological in his dealings within his own party.

The fate of the executive reorganization bill also illustrates this rising resentment. A modest measure for governmental reorganization, it was introduced about the same time as the court-packing bill (early 1937). It met with apathy, and in fact languished as all attention in the first half of that year focussed on the court fight. But in late 1937 it was taken up again and produced a popular and congressional outpouring of criticism of the president. Suddenly, it seemed, Roosevelt was seeking to become a dictator—he felt in fact obliged to issue a positive denial of such ambitions—through expanding his control of the government. Emotions were far out of touch with the realities of the proposed changes. And in April 1938 the president lost a measure that should have gone through Congress with little if any trouble. This was an indication of the changes taking place, of the split between the legislative and executive branches, and that also between more conservative and more liberal Democrats.

In a way the Democrats' own success under Roosevelt created part of their problem. The 1936 election had virtually destroyed the Republicans, increasing the likelihood that issues would be fought out inside the party in power. This was generally true in American politics, but especially so given the size of the new Democratic majority, and the inevitable variety that came to the party through its popularity in all parts of the country. Thus, in the Supreme Court battle the Republicans sat back and let the Democrats battle it out, only participating to support the anti-administration Democrats at the proper times. Given that more than 20 percent of members of the seventy-fifth Congress (1937–1939) were newcomers, often representing areas that had rarely gone Democratic before, it was hardly wise for the President to start off with so radical a step as the court packing plan. Intra-Democratic division was inevitable, to be sure, but Roosevelt's maneuvering tended to maximize it.

Beyond this, there were real issue differences over the legislative and administrative programs of the first term. The court-packing plan and its effects should not mask the fact that these differences were bound to emerge anyway. Relief and its vast expenditures, the Wagner Act, TVA, and Social Security—these and more were seen as radical by many Democrats, as was the increasing national power emanating from these programs and the president's way of administering them. Old line Democrats like Vice-President Garner, James F. Byrnes of South Carolina, and many more, represented very traditional social and economic ideas, and were offended by a New Deal ideology that went well beyond Roosevelt's own commitments before he entered office. Some of them, like Carter Glass of Virginia and Thomas Gore of Oklahoma, had consistently opposed the New Deal from the start. Others, like Byrnes and Millard Tydings of Maryland, increasingly joined them.

The labor violence of 1937 and 1938, most graphically demonstrated in the sit-down strikes, offended a broad spectrum of Americans. Not only was there violence and the apparent desecration of private property rights, but, more important, suddenly classes and class division seemed to have appeared in an America that had always prided itself on its classlessness. This was a powerful feeling among old stock, middle and lower-middle class groups like farmers, store owners, and so on, and their representatives in Congress were quite aware of and often shared their feelings.

Then came the recession of 1937–1938, which questioned even the efficacy of all that the New Deal had been doing. It was bad enough to engage in this radical legislation, these huge deficit budgets, this unprecedented federal interference in people's lives—but to do it all and not even have solved the economic problems that had triggered the New Deal seemed unbearable. It was not surprising that the House returned to committee the fair labor standards bill in late 1937, giving Roosevelt one of the most serious legislative defeats of his presidency; many members opposed to the bill on principle, and others were just growing wary of the whole process of legislating federal controls of American lives.

Certainly the southerners played a central role in the development of this new conservative coalition in Congress. The rapid expansion of federal power, and of the executive therein, violated traditional southern localism and stress on the legislative branch. Senator Bailey of North Carolina wrote to Senator Byrd of Virginia in the fall of 1937, that "what we have to do is to preserve, if we can, the Democratic party against his efforts to make it the Roosevelt party." The president's national popularity undercut the party per se, and especially the position of congressional leaders therein.

Southern fears were reinforced by the ideological bent of New Deal legislation. The agricultural legislation had not helped the south enough, they felt; relief moneys went too much to the cities; the labor legislation and especially minimum wage-maximum hours undercut the south's advantage in having cheaper labor costs, and threatened the stability of southern business. Moreover, the New Deal was a social threat, particularly in terms of race; both specific legislation and New Dealer commitments, and the general trend of the administration, seemed threatening to the system of racial segregation on which southern society was built. And so the most Democratic part of the nation grew increasingly opposed to the president.

Senator Bailey was a good example. He had been re-elected in 1936 as a New Deal supporter. This was partially a matter of belief, and also one of political necessity, since Roosevelt and the New Deal were generally popular in his state. But his reelection also gave him six years of security, from which advantage he was free to follow his conscience or his prejudices, as the case might be. He had always been bothered by the tremendous deficit spending of the New Deal, and high taxes and inflation disturbed him as well. The politics of relief and the rapid growth of the federal bureaucracy also concerned him, as did a growing sense that the New Dealers were different from himself, socially, intellectually, even in terms of feelings of what America was all about. Thus, he moved into opposition in 1937 and 1938, as did so many other, primarily southern Democrats. He opposed the court-packing plan, spoke openly against "radicals" like Harry Hopkins, and began to see, with others, that the dissident Democrats and the Republicans had a good deal in common, and some numbers as well.

One student of presidential-congressional relations during this period estimates that in 1937 the Senate had about eighteen Democrats, plus ten Republicans, who formed the core of the new conservative coalition. In the House it was about thirty Democrats and eighty Republicans. This alienation was seen in a House motion to investigate the sit-down strikes—a direct confrontation of administration policy. The measure was eventually beaten, 236–150, but 150 anti-administration votes was a significant total, especially when slightly over half were Democratic.

The president had called a special session of Congress in the fall of 1937, and it gave him none of what he asked for. This emboldened congressional conservatives for 1938. Congress was still, in its majority, pro-New Deal, but conservatives and moderates alike were more independent, more critical, more insistent in their own demands. South and north were clearly in conflict, as were rural and urban, old stock and new. The president had unprecedentedly difficult battles in both houses of Congress in 1938 over tax legislation, relief extension, fair labor standards, and executive reorganization. He scored 50–50 on these four major bills, which was far below his previous average.

Certainly by the early part of 1938 it was clear that the honeymoon was over. The unparalleled cooperation of executive and legislative branches, with the former clearly leading, had come to an end. The bowing of more conservative elements in the Democratic party to the ideological desires of the president was also over. The Democrats remained strong as a party, clearly in power; but their internal divisions raised questions about what they would be able to do with that power, and whether or not their coalition could hold.

These questions were not answered very clearly in 1938. Indeed, Roosevelt's disastrous effort to purge the party in the 1938 primaries only worsened—and at the same time reflected—the divisions in the party. But it is worth looking at the Purge in some detail, as a picture of the state of the party toward the end of the New Deal years.

The Purge was very much a Roosevelt decision and a Roosevelt action. When the topic was first discussed in 1937, most of the president's key advisers, including Farley and Flynn, opposed it. The president himself had generally avoided Democratic congressional primary battles in the past; in 1934 he had written to Key Pittman of Nevada that he regretted the "imposed silence in things like primaries," since he "wished to goodness I could speak out loud . . . that I am one thousand percent for you." Moreover, had the president been as close to the public temper as he was reputed to be, and often was, he would not have essayed so broad a purge in 1938. As with the court-packing plan, it clearly lacked a public mandate at the outset, and certainly lacked much approval as it fizzled to an end: 61 percent of the public expressed disapproval of the Purge in a fall, 1938 Gallup Poll. But here again is a sign that the president was a good deal more ideologically committed to the New Deal than is sometimes alleged; he often let ideology override purely political considerations, and this was one of the boldest and most divisive examples.

In fact the president's ideological insistence was not entirely an offensive one. He was under considerable pressure to defend the New Deal and the New Dealers by late 1937. Southern and other conservative Democrats had been urging him to purge such "radicals" as Ickes and Corcoran from his administration. And in his desire to defend such people, who were crucial to his domestic program, he had another reason to move against those who would have him do otherwise. As with the court battle, he was unduly impressed by the tremendous mandate he received from the voters in 1936, assuming that this meant the public would support him in an effort to mold the party more into his own image. But he ignored the strong thread of localism in America, the continuing commitment to separation of national and state affairs. And he failed to anticipate how local issues over which he had no control could motivate voters who were at the same time firmly committed to him and his administration.

Moreover, the president was emboldened by his earliest tentative efforts to influence the outcome of the 1938 primaries. In January, for example, he came out strongly in favor of Lister Hill in Alabama, running for the Senate seat vacated by Supreme Court Justice Hugo Black. Hill faced Thomas Heflin, a former Senator and long-time ultra-conservative, racist, and all-around bigot. Heflin had strong traditional support in the state, but Hill was able to confront it with equally strong administration, union, organized agricultural and establishment support, and won the primary with 65 percent of the vote. Much the same thing happened in Florida, where Claude Pepper sought re-election as an outspoken southern New Dealer. Pepper had lost a Senate race in 1934, but then had been elected in a special election two years later. Always a committed New Dealer, even if he had some disagreements with the president (e.g., FLSA), he made it clear to Floridians that "I am with Franklin D. Roosevelt and shall give him aggressive and helpful cooperation." He had strong conservative opposition for the May primary, but received equally strong administration support, not only in endorsements but also in terms of patronage and active involvement in Florida. He won easily, and gave Roosevelt another reason to believe that he really could affect the outcome of that year's primaries. The president did not stop to think that even if he were successful he might be seriously, even permanently dividing the party in the process.

Thus, Roosevelt pressed on, with victories and defeats, alienating some people regardless of the outcome. We have already seen how he was important in the defeat of New York Representative John O'Connor, Tammany man and conservative chairman of the House Rules Committee. FDR carefully selected his states and his contests. He backed off, for example, from challenging Bennett Champ Clark of Missouri or Augustine Lonergan of Connecticut, because the chances of success seemed slight; and was impressed by the fact that Lonergan at least responded to the threat to his tenure by speaking more favorably of the New Deal by the summer of the year.

Moreover, Roosevelt's actions were not always divisive. In Illinois the continuing battle between the Kelly-Nash and Horner factions of the party once more tended to involve the president. Roosevelt decided on a hands-off policy, even though incumbent Senator Dietrich's vote had been crucial in Barkley's election to the leadership of the Senate. While this was hardly fair to Dietrich it did conciliate the two factions. Much the same happened in Pennsylvania where Roosevelt tried to deal even-handedly with both the Guffey and the Earle-Lawrence factions of the party.

The Purge itself was relatively successful in the midwest and west. In Kentucky, for example, he arrived in the summer to try to save Senator Barkley from the challenge of Governor A. B. "Happy" Chandler. Chandler was not greatly anti-New Deal, although he had little sympathy with organized labor; but Barkley as Senate Majority Leader, was a key member of the New Deal team, and his loss might well result in the more conservative Pat Harrison replacing him. Roosevelt spoke in Kentucky for Barkley, patronage through the WPA was increased, other assistance was given, and Barkley won the August Democratic primary with 57 percent of the vote.

Oregon was somewhat similar, although less clear. Its governor, Charles H. Martin, was a very conservative Democrat who had resisted the New Deal nationally and in his state. He was opposed in the primary by Henry Hess, who had strong liberal and labor support inside the state. Martin was endorsed by Farley—the professional politician always focussing on the health of the party—but Hess got his support from Senator Norris, Harold Ickes, and, implicity, the president. Hess won a narrow primary victory, and it was seen as a victory for Roosevelt as well.

The president was less in control, however, in Iowa, Incumbent Senator Gillette was acceptable to FDR, but James Roosevelt, Ickes, and others preferred Congressman Otha Wearin, and got Hopkins to endorse him also. Roosevelt was embarrassed by the whole situation and stayed out of it. But Gillette's strong victory was despite New Deal opposition and made the president appear somehow out of touch. And in Indiana he appeared almost overwhelmed. Senator Frederick Van Nuys had moved into opposition to the New Deal on the major issues of 1937–1938, and was also split from the Indiana Democratic organization of Paul V. McNutt; both sides wanted to dump him. But Van Nuys fought against it, announcing that he would run as an independent if he did not get the Democratic nomination. He brought in Burton K. Wheeler, leader of the anti-court-packing forces, and threatened to bring in additional conservative Democratic senators if necessary. Pushing his advantage, Van Nuys insisted that if there were any opponents against him at all in the primary he would avoid it and run anyway. The state and national leaders caved in completely, and Van Nuys had his triumph. FDR had been far too overconfident about the ability of a local Democratic organization to control the state, an overconfidence that emanated from his assumption that the pro-New Deal faction would always be the one with the greatest popular support.

Elsewhere in the west the president fared pretty well in his travels and interjections in the summer of 1938. Ohio, Arkansas, Oklahoma— all saw New Deal victories of sorts. But in Texas the president's strong support of liberal Maury Maverick was not enough to keep him from losing renomination to the House. And in the cases of Senator Alva Adams of Colorado, who was only moderate in his opposition to the New Deal, and Senator Pat McCarran of Nevada, the president had to cave in before the primaries, nonetheless leaving hurt feelings behind.

Arkansas was another administration victory in the south. Mrs. Hattie Caraway confronted Congressman John McClellan, a firm opponent of New Deal legislation. It would not be easy to elect a woman to the U. S. Senate from Arkansas, but Roosevelt took her on his train through Arkansas, spoke well of her, and ignored McClellan; she won the primary with slightly over fifty-one percent of the vote. But in South Carolina, on the other hand, the president was overwhelmed. True, Senator "Cotton Ed" Smith was a leading New Deal opponent, and a virulent racist as well, but he was too strong in the state, and Hopkins and other administration officials advised the president to stay out. FDR ignored their advice and supported the young governor, Olin

Johnston. Smith fought back, arguing that the Purge was really a battle against white supremacy; it was an argument that found a receptive audience in South Carolina, and the senator received 55 percent of the primary vote. Maryland was little better; despite the president giving several speeches for his opponent, conservative Senator Millard Tydings swept the primary with 60 percent of the vote.

Georgia was even worse. Roosevelt had been successful there in 1936, helping incumbent Richard Russell fight off the challenge of Eugene Talmadge. Moreover, the governor, E. D. Rivers, was also a strong New Dealer. Thus it did not seem unwise to try to defeat Walter F. George, who had been in the Senate since 1922 and had turned against the New Deal in 1937. The contest was complicated by the fact that Talmadge was also an announced candidate, and equally unpalatable to the president. Roosevelt ignored the warnings of Farley and others and settled on Lawrence Camp, who was not well known and really had little chance; the president came to Georgia and spoke out for his chosen candidate, at a meeting attended by George and Talmadge as well. He also put patronage into the contest on Camp's behalf. But George responded with a general oratorical support of the New Deal (he called himself an "80 percent New Dealer") and a strong insistence on local control of local affairs. It became an issue of Georgians rather than outsiders deciding who should represent Georgia, and on that basis there was little vocal support in the state for the president's choice. Even Governor Rivers and Senator Russell refused to get involved. Camp ran as an out-and-out New Dealer, but it was just not enough. George received 44 percent, to 32 percent for Talmadge and 24 percent for Camp. The president was humbled.

It is difficult to total up the administration's wins and losses in the Purge simply because there is no agreement on which contests ought to be included. Sometimes he was just shoring up a challenged but nonetheless favored incumbent; other times he was trying to replace an incumbent with a more supportive rival. Certainly there were successes; but even if they outnumbered the failures, it was the failures that counted. They intensified the division in the party. Those whom Roosevelt tried to defeat but did not, in addition to those who sympathized with them on ideological or purely partisan bases, comprised a formidable force in the party from that time forward.

The Purge was a mistake for several reasons. Tactically, it was not well run. In the west, for example, the president just passed through, supporting this candidate and opposing that one. He did not really conduct any type of follow-up, assuming too often that the local New Deal party organization would accomplish that. But this was hard to do, and even where the purging was successful, a divided state party organization was left behind. Beyond that, there were too many Democrats in the country who felt that party welfare required incumbent party members to always be supported, and more who felt that there were definite limits to the acceptable level of federal interference in local party affairs.

It is important to understand that the Purge was as much an effect of party division as it was a cause. That division was already clear by early 1938. But the Purge played its role in exacerbating it, complicating the party's position for that year's general elections, and even more helping to end the unusual party harmony that had marked the first Roosevelt administration.

Beyond the aforementioned, there were a variety of other factors that led to a decline in administration and Democratic popularity at the end of the 1930s. People were generally concerned about the new power of government and the size of the national bureaucracy. There was good reason to argue that all the programs and all the expenditures had not solved the nation's economic problems, and unemployment remained high. Certainly the recession of 1937–1938 was reason for concern; even Roosevelt was not persuaded of the validity of the Keynesian argument that too little spending, rather than too much, had caused the decline. It was probably true that more New Deal, not less, was one key to recovery, but few were ready for it at that time. There were also foreign policy fears, and failures, that were beginning to persuade Americans that their government was not doing all that well, and might even be en route to pulling the country into another European war. The decade, moreover, witnessed a great deal of ethnic and religious antagonism; fascism had its supporters, anti-semitism had more, and both suggested that Roosevelt and the New Deal were prime enemies.

Given all this, the Republican resurgence, and even broader conservative renewal of 1938 were not really surprising. We have seen in earlier chapters the nature of this Democratic and New Deal loss in 1938. It tended to be general, and thus did not really disrupt the basis of the Democratic coalition. But it was nonetheless serious, especially in the northeast and west. After the election there were still 69 Democrats out of the 96 members of the Senate, but about one-third of those 69 were hostile to the New Deal. There were also eight new Republicans there, six of whom had defeated pro-New Deal Democrats. The

House was similar; the number of Republicans doubled, as eighty-two Democrats were defeated, and the House was now over one-third Republican. About a dozen Democratic governorships were also lost.

Some of these losses were real individual blows to the president. Governor Frank Murphy of Michigan, for example, was a New Deal stalwart, whom Roosevelt had urged to run for that office in 1936 to strengthen the party. And the Democrats had developed real strength in that traditionally Republican state. Murphy had been a New Deal governor, strongly identified with liberalism generally and unionism in particular; he gained national notoriety for his refusal to use force against the sitdown strikers, making their ultimate success possible. But the result in Michigan was that he forfeited the support of much of the rest of the population, at the same time as general anti-New Deal sentiment was growing. Murphy lost his 1938 bid for reelection, both houses of the state legislature also went Republican, and the Democrats remained strong only in the industrial cities.

The 1938 elections launched the careers of some major Republican names of the ensuing twenty years—Bricker, Dewey, Stassen, Mundt, Taft. These were the people, along with conservative, primarily southern Democrats, who would lead the opposition to any expansion of the New Deal down to the 1960s.

The vote showed the diffidence of the people. And Congress, in refusing to respond to Roosevelt's initiatives in 1938, 1939, and after, reflected the people's wishes and public opinion generally—up to a point. The public was afraid of too much government, too much activism, too much class division. The polls did show less enthusiasm for imaginative legislative solutions than in the past. But this did not mean that there was mass support for undoing what had already been accomplished, although the anti-New Dealers jumped to that conclusion, which seriously limited their ability to play other than a limiting and negative role in American politics.

Strangely, just as the White House was losing much of its influence and control over Congress, it was establishing a new and long-lasting pro-New Deal majority on the Supreme Court. In a way this influence was more important. The New Deal had done almost all of its legislative work in the first term; what was then necessary for this program to survive and be implemented was court support and approval. The court did approve, and the New Deal survived. The rise of the conservative coalition in Congress only halted its expansion, not its effect.

For that matter, the Democrats remained the overwhelming majority in Congress after the 1938 elections. And although they disagreed on many important issues, they agreed on others, particularly those partisan matters so crucial to the party's general strength. Not until 1948 did the party really split on the national level—and in that election it was both the ultraconservatives and the ultraliberals who left, without impeding Harry S Truman's success. On the other hand, the Republicans, even though a small minority, were far from united. The party conservatives who insisted on no response to the New Deal other than nay-saying were contested by moderates who felt the party could never bounce back to power unless it modernized itself and came to terms with those aspects of the New Deal that the public seemed insistent on. The Republican compromises of Willkie in 1940, Dewey in 1944 and 1948, and for that matter Eisenhower in 1952 and 1956, recognized the fact that the party continued divided and unable to take a strong ideological position that had any chance of disrupting the New Deal coalition.

The era of the Depression, the New Deal, and Franklin D. Roosevelt had profound effects on American politics, certainly for a generation, and in many respects down to the present. In no area was this effect more clear and more important than that of popular voting behavior. The New Deal coalition of the South, the cities, and the poor and working class generally, including numerous national, racial, and religious minority groups, was the strongest majority coalition in modern American history. It obliterated and replaced the majority Republican coalition that had lasted from the mid-1890s to the end of 1920s. And the Democratic era thus created has changed the nature of American politics in other ways: never before had the poor and the urban had as much power as they did from the 1930s on, hardly unlimited, but nonetheless including far greater access to and influence over national government and policy than at any time since the first part of the nineteenth century.

The breadth and resilience of this coalition has been striking. Through three major wars and two eight-year Republican presidencies the Democrats have remained clearly the majority party. The Republicans managed to capture control of Congress only in the immediate postwar and nonpresidential election of 1946, and again at the time of the first Eisenhower victory in 1952. But Truman's unexpected victory in 1948 showed the commitment of the public to the New Deal generally. And Eisenhower's failure to carry either house of Congress for his party in 1956 (the first time that had happened in modern American history) showed the close relationship of that public commitment to one also to the Democrats as a party.

Since that time Congress has remained Democratic. Another elected Republican president fared no better. And recently, while some observers are impressed with the extent to which the New Deal coalition may be breaking down, it is equally impressive to see how strong it is, and how, forty years after the end of the New Deal, the Republicans are if anything a less acceptable partisan alternative than they were before.

State and local voting have been only slightly less consistent than national. Particularly in the cities, where local government has, through New Deal programs and their successors, become increasingly tied in to and dependent on national government, the Democrats continue to exercise control. Moreover, as the cities have become increasingly dominated, demographically, by those economic, social, and cultural groups that have the greatest connection to the Democratic party, there exists yet another reason for this control. State government, on the other hand, has become somewhat less significant, and has shown greater partisan variation. This is particularly true in the south, where racial crisis led to some redevelopment of the Republican party. But it has not led to any important changes in national voting among most southerners. And the conservative coalition itself disintegrated in the late 1960s, rendered inoperable by social change in the south.

The New Deal coalition began to break down in the 1960s, logically enough since the successes of the New Deal resulted in many Americans moving out of the socioeconomic position that had made them so sympathetic to it in the first place. But the breakdown has been not to another party; rather it has been to greater nonpartisanship. It is impossible to predict whether the breakdown will continue. Certainly the New Deal coalition has already lasted longer than any other in American history. For the time being, however, even if it has become a weaker coalition than it once was, it remains the only one around— that is some measure of the depth of the popular voting change that took place in the 1930s.

We have also seen that the New Deal years resulted in a tremendous increase in the size and scope of government generally, particularly national government. This has influenced American politics in that people demand more from it than they ever did before. In our day people expect, as natural, that government can deal with social, cultural, and attitudinal problems, as well as with straightforward political and economic ones. Small wonder, then, that there is heightened dissatisfaction with government and political parties generally, when they are asked to resolve things traditionally seen as private before the age of FDR.

Along with the rise of government came the rise of the presidency, to an influence and power greater than ever before. What Roosevelt achieved here—partly out of the situation, partly from desire—has not diminished; rather, the contrary has resulted. One speaks today of an "imperial presidency," and the nation witnessed in the early 1970s a major constitutional crisis where, had the president not backed down and resigned in ignominy, the question of presidential vs. legislative vs. judicial power might have paralyzed the nation. The office increased its power because both the situation and the people seemed to demand it. Neither of these sources has yet diminished.

But in the process the presidency became less partisan to some degree. Voting for the presidency and for other offices were always somewhat distinct from one another, and this became even more true after the New Deal. This fact explains the closeness of the Republican-Democratic split in presidential voting, and even the four Republican presidential election victories, existing amidst a continued overwhelming national Democratic popularity. Thus, the increased power of the office has also meant its removal from part of its traditional partisan role and strength.

The New Deal also established a set of ideological mandates and limits that have proved quite resilient. The overwhelming defeats of Barry Goldwater in 1964 and George McGovern in 1972 suggest the right-wing and left-wing limits of these guidelines. And the general failure of the Republicans as a party has shown the extent to which the Democrats have done a far better job of learning the lesson of the 1930s than have their opponents. For the New Deal, in a moderate and bourgeois sense, committed American government to important changes in our system of political economy. Hardly perfect, indeed far from even being well-implemented, they nonetheless argued that there were bare minima of living standards beneath which members of the society were not permitted to go; that those with the greatest wealth had traditionally possessed too much of it and too much power, and that support should come from government to individuals and organizations that sought to counter this tradition; that those Americans closely identified with distinct ethnic, racial, or religious minority positions deserved full equality and opportunity while not being obliged to sacrifice their traditions; that American society had for too long been insensitive to the injustices and inequalities that had persisted within it despite an official national commitment to the contrary.

Skeptics can well point to the fact that these problems were not always confronted directly by Roosevelt or the New Deal, and to the extent to which these inequities were by no means undone then, or since. They can properly argue that the wealth of the society, and certainly its power as well, are by no means yet evenly distributed; that social and economic and ethnic conflict still exist, and that invidious distinctions continue. But this does not negate, it seems to me, the importance of the New Deal in being the first American administration to try to confront these problems, to directly admit their existence, and to try to do something about them. Sometimes it was the president himself who took the lead, more often it was bolder ideologues in the administration or politicians outside of it, but in sum an effort to truly humanize American government and render it responsive to all the people was undertaken.

This is nowhere clearer than in the response of the American people to the New Deal. In the record-breaking commitment of so many groups of Americans, particularly the less privileged, to the party of the New Deal and Franklin Roosevelt one sees not blind trust nor unsophisticated overexpectation. Rather, one senses a rational appraisal of where the possibilities for the future lay. The Democratic era that dawned in the 1930s did not create a just society in America, but it did bring a politics seeking a juster society than the nation had known before.

Appendix

In these few pages I want to provide the reader with a more systematic description of the materials and methods of the quantitative aspects of this book. If quantitative techniques are to be useful and reliable, whether elementary or advanced, it is essential that the writer be unambiguous and complete. Quantitative materials, like more traditional ones, require documentation and substantiation; also like more traditional materials, they are only as useful and creative as the scholar makes them.

The Data

The data comprise two machine-readable files prepared by the Inter-University Consortium for Political and Social Research (ICPSR). The largest and most important of the files was of data aggregated by county, for all the counties in the United States (presently 3426 in number, in the 1930s about 3100). The file contained about 145 variables, or items of information, for each county, or case. This gave a total of about 450,000 items of information (actually closer to 550,000 after I created new variables from old ones), a large file.

The file contained two distinct kinds of data. The first were voting data, the total vote per county for each major and important minor party for the presidential elections of 1932 and 1936, and the House of Representatives elections of 1930, 1932, 1934, 1936, 1938. The second kind of data, comprising two-thirds of the variables, was 1930 census data (plus a few items gathered in 1937), giving county totals on a wide variety of measures. These included population data (e.g., sex, race, nativity, schooling), residential data (e.g., urban, rural, population per square mile), employment data (e.g., employed, unemployed, kinds of work, salaries), and other economic data (e.g., size of farms, sales, manufactures). Some of these variables I recalculated or combined to create more useful ones (e.g., dividing many variables by total population to get a percentage rather than raw figure, combining foreign born and their children to get foreign stock).

The second file, much smaller, was voting, by state, for governor and United States Senator, for major and important minor parties, 1930–1938. This was used primarily in Chapter 5.

The main quantitative problem of the book resulted from the nature of the data. Counties were the smallest feasible unit for such a national study: data for smaller units was less readily available, and my 3100+ cases comprises an already very large data base even for a computer. But counties are for many purposes not ideal units. This is primarily because they are too populous to permit careful analysis of the effects of individual social, economic, or other characteristics on political behavior. If we are interested, for example, in the relationship between foreign birth, or unemployment, or race, and voting for the Democrats in a given election, we have real difficulties because the size and heterogeneity of counties makes it very difficult to see the effect of such variables. The kinds of relationships one can see clearly in looking at the precincts or sometimes even the wards of a city, just are not possible with data aggregated at the county level.

Beyond that, since counties are created by the states, neither their number nor their boundaries need conform to any national standard. The south, for example, which made up only 21 percent of the total national population in 1930, had at the same time over one-third of the total number of counties. Similar, albeit smaller, discrepancies existed in other states and groups of states as well. Thus, whenever one calculates, let us say, a national average, when the unit of analysis is the county, the result is bound to be highly overinfluenced by the south; and since that area was distinctive in so many ways (e.g., overwhelmingly Democratic, more rural and black, etc.) the results of the calculations will be of marginal value. This is why I have almost always presented data on a regional basis: that does not resolve the problem entirely, but it makes the data less misleading.

The county-based nature of the data was its main weakness, but not the only one. The census does not always ask the questions we would like to have answers to; union membership, for example, would have been a very useful variable. And the census does not always classify its information as we would like it; the census definition of "urban" as a place of 2500 or more residents results in a measure of urban residence that is not really very useful.

Thus, as I noted in the Preface, the data and their manipulation in this book comprise more a suggestive kind of information than precise description or analysis. This was an inevitable compromise, and one which I decided was justifiable. If I have often been unhappy with many of the outcomes of my calculations—finding neither positive confirmation nor denial of my own or others' generalizations—I remain convinced that what I have is worthwhile, and contributes to my analysis of the political effects of the New Deal. Other scholars, impressed or offended by what they see here, will solve some of these problems in the future, and provide greater certitude and more impressive analysis.

For the purposes of this book, it is important for readers to realize the limitations imposed by the data. From that they can draw their own conclusions of the persuasiveness of my interpretations of it.

Statistics and Method

Beyond the question of the data itself, there remains that of what I did with it. The statistical manipulations themselves are fairly straightforward, and were done with *Statistical Package for the Social Sciences* programs. I have used primarily percentages, which are simple, clear, and often sufficient. By using the computer to isolate counties that were high or low on any given characteristic or set of characteristics (e.g., more urban, or southern, or foreign born) and comparing those counties to others, I sought to find suggestions of the effect of individual variables, especially on voting behavior. This is a rather imprecise measure, but given the limitations of the data was often about as good as I could get. It is also easy to follow.

I have used correlation coefficients, specifically the Pearson product moment coefficient (r), because they are a more precise analytical and descriptive tool. This measure, r, is widely used, especially with percentaged data, to gauge the strength of relationship between two variables. It measures relationship, not causation, although the latter may be inferred. It really shows the extent to which we can predict, knowing the value of one variable, the likely value of the other. Given an independent variable (e.g., percent foreign born) and a dependent one (e.g., percent voting for Roosevelt in 1932), the calculation of r measures the extent to which an increase in the one is accompanied by an increase or decrease in the other, for all of the cases (here, counties) involved. An r value, or coefficient, of 1.00 shows perfect positive correlation, with all cases increasing to the same degree on one variable with increases to the same degree on the other variable (really, that all points of the scattergram fall directly on the least squares line). Conversely, a value for r of −1.00 (the opposite extreme) shows that, to an equal degree, increases on one variable are accompanied by decreases on the other.

Thus, in the example above, an r value of .750 between foreign birth and voting for Roosevelt would show quite strong association or relationship between the two (statistically, it says that knowing the value of the first, we could confidently predict from that information alone 56% of the total value of the second). Conversely, a value of −.750 between being old stock and voting for Roosevelt would tell us just about the same thing. Positive and negative correlations are equally significant; it is their strength that we are most concerned with. There is no absolute criterion for what is or is not a meaningful value for r. This depends on many things, especially the nature of the data. Given that our data is county level, where independent variables tend to get lost because of the size of the counties, we simply cannot obtain the level of correlation one finds when dealing, for example, with city precincts, which are far more homogeneous. The result is that my correlations are less analytically precise and satisfactory than I would have liked; I have had to settle for lower levels of relationship, and have accepted them as suggestive rather than authoritative. Nonetheless r is a very useful and, once understood, clear measure of association between two variables, and thus I have used it in a number of places.

The regional divisions I used in this study are the standard ICPSR ones, with an added control on county population size. Thus, for the "urban northeast," I used all counties in the New England, Middle

Atlantic, and East North Central regions that had populations of 250,000 or more. For "nonurban south" I used all counties in the ten-state Solid South with populations less than 250,000; the same population norm was used for "nonurban midwest" (the West North Central region) and "nonurban mountain" (the Mountain region). In Chapter 4, for urban areas, I used all counties in the United States with populations in excess of 500,000 population.

In a number of places in the book, I have divided independent variables into two or more categories (e.g., low foreign stock–high foreign stock; low percentage of workers in manufacturing–medium percentage of workers in manufacturing–high percentage of workers in manufacturing; etc.), and looked at the varying levels of Democratic voting for each category, nationally or for regions. The development of those categories was primarily by trial and error. I had to take into consideration regional variations, making the original divisions nontenable sometimes if based on national averages. I also found that a "purely statistical" division (e.g., with the middle category one standard deviation to each side of the mean, and the lower and upper categories the remainder) also did not always work, because of skewed distributions and sometimes insufficient cases for a category. Thus I ran the data over and over until I had categories that involved enough cases (this is why there are sometimes three categories and sometimes two), and which seemed to me reasonable and indicative. Once again, I opted for some sort of meaningful description rather than for statistical rigor. Readers who might be interested in any specific variable(s), and how I categorized them, or who are concerned with any aspects of the quantitative data, are welcome to correspond directly with me.

Bibliography

Allswang, John M., "The Chicago Negro Voter and the Democratic Consensus," *Illinois State Historical Society Journal,* 50 (1967).

——, *A House for All Peoples: Ethnic Politics in Chicago,* 1890–1936, University Press of Kentucky, Lexington, 1971.

Astorino, Samuel J., "The Decline of the Republican Dynasty in Pennsylvania, 1929–1934," unpublished doctoral dissertation, University of Pittsburgh, Pittsburgh, 1962.

Bailey, Robert J., "Theodore G. Bilbo and the Sensational Election of 1934," *Southern Quarterly,* 10 (1971).

Bain, George W., "How Negro Editors Viewed the New Deal," *Journalism Quarterly,* 44 (1967).

Bernstein, Irving, *The Lean Years: A History of the American Worker, 1920–1933,* Houghton-Mifflin, Boston, 1960.

——, *Turbulent Years: A History of the American Worker, 1933–1941,* Houghton-Mifflin, Boston, 1970.

Betten, Neil, "Catholic Periodicals in Response to Two Divergent Decades," *Journalism Quarterly,* 47 (1970).

Billington, Monroe, "Sen. Thomas P. Gore," *Chronicles of Oklahoma,* 35 (1957).

Blackorby, Edward C., *Prairie Rebel: The Public Life of William Lemke,* University of Nebraska Press, Lincoln, 1963.

——, "William Lemke: Agrarian Radical and Union Party Presidential Candidate," *Mississippi Valley Historical Review,* 49 (1962).

Bone, Hugh, "Political Parties in New York City," *American Political Science Review,* 40 (1946).

Boorstin, Daniel J., "Selling the President to the People," *Commentary,* 20 (1955).

Boskin, Joseph, *Opposition Politics: the Anti-New Deal Tradition,* The Glencoe Press, Beverly Hills, Calif., 1968.

——, "Politics of an Opposition Party: the Republican Party in the New Deal Period, 1936-1940," unpublished doctoral dissertation, University of Minnesota, Minneapolis, 1959.

Braeman, John, Robert H. Bremner, and David Brody, *The New Deal,* 2 vols., Ohio State University Press, Columbus, 1975.

Brewer, James H., "Robert Lee Vann, Democrat or Republican: An Exponent of Loose Leaf Politics," *Negro History Bulletin,* 21 (1958).

Bronner, Edwin B., "The New Deal Comes to Pennsylvania: the Gubernatorial Election of 1934," *Pennsylvania History,* 27 (1960).

Burke, Robert E., *Olson's New Deal for California,* University of California Press, Berkeley and Los Angeles, 1953.

Burner, David, *The Politics of Provincialism: the Democratic Party in Transistion, 1918-1932,* Knopf, New York, 1968.

Burns, James MacGregor, *Roosevelt: the Lion and the Fox,* Harcourt Brace Jovanovich, New York, 1956.

Bussel, Alan, "The Fight Against Boss Crump: Editor Meeman's Turn," *Journalism Quarterly,* 44 (1967).

Calbert, Jack L., "James Edward and Miriam Amanda Ferguson: the 'Ma' and 'Pa' of Texas Politics," unpublished doctoral dissertation, Indiana University, Bloomington, 1968.

Cann, Marvin, "Burnett Maybank and Charleston Politics in the New Deal Era," *Proceedings of the South Carolina Historical Assn.* (1970).

——, "The End of a Political Myth: the South Carolina Gubernatorial Campaign of 1938," *South Carolina History Magazine,* 72 (1971).

Cantril, Hadley, *Public Opinion, 1935-1946,* Princeton University Press, Princeton, 1951.

Carleton, William G., "The Revolution in the Presidential Nominating Convention," *Political Science Quarterly,* 72 (1957).

Coker, William S., "Pat Harrison—Strategy for Victory," *Journal of Mississippi History,* 28 (1966).

Collins, Ernest, "Cincinnati Negroes and Presidential Politics," *Journal of Negro History,* 41 (1956).

Conkin, Paul, *The New Deal,* Crowell, New York, 1967.

Connors, Richard J., *A Cycle of Power: the Career of Jersey City Mayor Frank Hague,* The Scarecrow Press, Metuchen, N.J., 1971.

Coode, Thomas H., "The Presidential Election of 1940 as Reflected in the Tennessee Metropolitan Press," *East Tennessee Historical Society Publications,* 40 (1968).

Cornwell, Elmer E., "The Presidential Press Conference: A Study in Institutionalization," *Midwest Journal of Political Science,* 4 (1960).

Cox, E. F., *State and National Voting,* Archon Books, Hamden, Conn., 1972.

Cox, Merlin G., "David Sholtz: New Deal governor of Florida," *Florida Historical Quarterly,* 43 (1964).

Cummings, Milton C., Jr., *Congressmen and the Electorate: Elections for the U. S. House and the President, 1920-1964,* The Free Press New York, 1966.

Davis, James W., *Presidential Primaries: Road to the White House,* Crowell, New York, 1967.

Dorsett, Lyle W., *The Pendergast Machine,* Oxford University Press, New York, 1968.

Dunn, Larry W., "Knoxville Negro Voting and the Roosevelt Revolution, 1928-1936," *East Tennessee Historical Society Publications,* 43 (1971).

Eldersveld, Samuel J., "The Influence of Metropolitan Party Pluralities in Presidential Elections since 1920: A Study of Twelve Key Cities," *American Political Science Review,* 43 (1949).

Farley, James A., *Behind the Ballots: the Personal History of a Politician,* Harcourt Brace Jovanovich, New York, 1938.

———, *Jim Farley's Story: the Roosevelt Years,* McGraw-Hill, New York, 1948.

Fleming, Thomas J., "The Political Machine II: a Case History: 'I Am the Law,'" *American Heritage,* 20 (1969).

Flynn, Edward J., *You're the Boss,* Viking, New York, 1947.

Fossett, Roy E., "The Impact of the New Deal on Georgia Politics, 1933-1941," unpublished doctoral dissertation, University of Florida, Gainesville, 1960.

Freidel, Frank, *Franklin D. Roosevelt,* IV: *Launching the New Deal,* Little, Brown, Boston, 1973.

———, *F.D.R. and the South,* Louisiana State University Press, Baton Rouge, 1965.

———, *The New Deal and the American People,* Prentice-Hall, Englewood Cliffs, N.J., 1964.

Fuchs, Lawrence H., "American Jews and the Presidential Vote," *American Political Science Review,* 49 (1955).

Fuller, John F., "The Press and the 1938 North Dakota Election," *North Dakota History,* 35 (1968).

Gallup, George H., *The Gallup Poll, 1935–1971,* Random House, New York, 1972.

Garrett, Charles, *The LaGuardia Years: Machine and Reform Politics in New York City,* Rutgers University Press, New Brunswick, N. J., 1961.

Gelfand, Mark I., *A Nation of Cities: the Federal Government and Urban America, 1933–1965,* Oxford University Press, New York, 1975.

Gordon, Rita W., "The Change in the Political Alignment of Chicago's Negroes During the New Deal," *Journal of American History,* 56 (1969).

Gosnell, Harold F., *Champion Campaigner: Franklin D. Roosevelt,* Macmillan, New York, 1952.

———, "Does Campaigning Make a Difference?" *Public Opinion Quarterly,* 14 (1950).

Graebner, Norman A., "Depression and Urban Votes," *Current History,* 23 (1952).

Green, Fletcher M., "Resurgent Southern Sectionalism, 1933–1955," *North Carolina Historical Review,* 33 (1956).

Halt, Charles E., "Joseph F. Guffey, New Deal Politician form Pennsylvania," unpublished doctoral dissertation, Syracuse University, Syracuse, 1965.

Harrell, James A., "Negro Leadership in the Election Year 1936," *Journal of Southern History,* 34 (1968).

Hayes, Robert E., "Senatorial Voting Behavior with Regard to the 'Southern Interest,'" unpublished doctoral dissertation, University of Colorado, Boulder, 1964.

Hopper, John E., "The Purge: Franklin D. Roosevelt and the 1938 Democratic Nominations," unpublished doctoral dissertation, University of Chicago, Chicago, 1966.

Huthmacher, J. Joseph, *Massachusetts People and Politics, 1919-1933,* Atheneum, New York, 1969.

Jones, Gene Delon, "The Local Political Significance of New Deal Relief Legislation in Chicago, 1933-1940," unpublished doctoral dissertation, Northwestern University, Evanston, Illinois, 1970.

Kearnes, John, "Utah Electoral Politics, 1932-1938," unpublished doctoral dissertation, University of Utah, Provo, 1972.

Kearns, Doris, *Lyndon Johnson and the American Dream,* Harper, New York, 1976.

Kehl, James A., and Samuel J. Astorino, "A Bull Moose Responds to the New Deal: Pennsylvania's Gifford Pinchot," *Pennsylvania Magazine of History and Biography,* 88 (1964).

Lapomarda, Vincent A., "Maurice Joseph Tobin; the Decline of Bossism in Boston," *New England Quarterly,* 43 (1970).

Larsen, Charles E., "The EPIC Campaign of 1934," *Pacific Historical Review,* 27 (1958).

Larson, T. A., "The New Deal in Wyoming," *Pacific Historical Review,* 38 (1969).

Leuchtenberg, William E., *Franklin D. Roosevelt and the New Deal, 1932-1940,* Harper, New York, 1963.

Ludwig, E. Jeffrey, "Pennsylvania: the National Election of 1932," *Pennsylvania History,* 31 (1964).

Lunt, Richard, "Frank Murphy's Decision to Enter the 1936 Gubernatorial Race," *Michigan History,* 47 (1963).

McCoy, Donald R., "The Formation of the Wisconsin Progressive Party in 1934," *Historian,* 14 (1951).

———, "The National Progressives of America, 1938," *Mississippi Valley Historical Review,* 44 (1957).

———, "The Progressive National Committee of 1936," *Western Political Quarterly,* 9 (1956).

McKean, Dayton D., *The Boss: the Hague Machine in Action,* Houghton-Mifflin, Boston, 1940.

MacRae, Duncan, Jr., and J. A. Meldrum, "Critical Elections in Illinois, 1888-1958," *American Political Science Review,* 54 (1960).

McSeveney, Samuel T., "The Michigan Gubernatorial Campaign of 1938," *Michigan History,* 45 (1961).

Malone, Michael P., *C. Ben Ross and the New Deal in Idaho,* University of Washington Press, Seattle, 1970.

———, "Montana Politics in the New Deal," *Montana,* 21 (1971).

———, "The New Deal in Idaho," *Pacific Historical Review,* 38 (1969).

Marcello, Ronald E., "The North Carolina Works Progress Administration and the Politics of Relief," unpublished doctoral dissertation, Duke University, Durham, 1968.

Martin, Charles H., "Negro Leaders, the Republican Party, and the Election of 1932," *Phylon*, 32 (1971).

Massey, Robert K., Jr., "The Democratic Laggard: Massachusetts in 1932," *New England Quarterly*, 44 (1971).

Mazuzan, George T., "Vermont's Traditional Republicanism vs. the New Deal," *Vermont History*, 39 (1971).

Miller, William D., "The Browning-Crump Battle: the Crump Side," *East Tennessee Historical Society Publications*, 37 (1965).

Mooney, Booth, *Roosevelt and Rayburn: a Political Friendship*, Lippincott, Philadelphia, 1971.

O'Brien, David J., *American Catholics and Social Reform: the New Deal Years*, Oxford University Press, New York, 1968.

Ogburn, William F., and Lolagene C. Coombs, "The Economic Factors in Roosevelt Elections," *American Political Science Review*, 34 (1940).

O'Rourke, Paul A., "South Dakota Politics during the New Deal Years," *South Dakota History*, 1 (1971).

Ortquist, Richard T., Jr., "Depression Politics in Michigan: the Election of 1932," *Michigan Academician*, 2 (1970).

Overacker, Louise, *Presidential Campaign Funds*, Boston University Press, Boston, 1946.

Patterson, James T., *Congressional Conservatism and the New Deal: the Growth of the Conservative Coalition in Congress, 1933–1939*, University of Kentucky Press, Lexington, 1967.

——, "The Failure of Party Realignment in the South, 1937–1939," *Journal of Politics*, 27 (1965).

——, *The New Deal and the States: Federalism in Transition*, Princeton University Press, Princeton, 1969.

——, "The New Deal and the West," *Pacific Historical Review*, 38 (1969).

Paul, Justus F., "The Ku Klux Klan in the Midwest: a Note on the 1936 Nebraska Elections," *North Dakota Quarterly*, 39 (1971).

Plesur, Milton, "The Republican Congressional Comeback of 1938," *Review of Politics*, 24 (1962).

Polenberg, Richard, "Franklin Roosevelt and the Purge of John O'Connor: the Impact of Urban Change on Political Parties," *New York History*, 49 (1968).

Pollard, James E., "The White House News Conference as a Channel of Communication," *Public Opinion Quarterly,* 15 (1951).

Powell, David O., "The Union Party of 1936: Campaign Tactics and Issues," *Mid-America,* 46 (1964).

———, "The Union Party of 1936: Organization and Finance," *North Dakota History,* 34 (1967).

Price, Charles M., and Joseph Boskin, "The Roosevelt Purge: a Reappraisal," *Journal of Politics,* 28 (1966).

Ragland, James F., "Franklin D. Roosevelt and Public Opinion, 1933–1940," unpublished doctoral dissertation, Stanford University, Stanford, Calif., 1954.

———, "Merchandisers of the First Amendment: Freedom and Responsibility of the Press in the Age of Roosevelt, 1933–1940," *Georgia Review,* 16 (1962).

Robinson, Edgar E., *They Voted for Roosevelt: the Presidential Vote, 1932–1940,* Stanford University Press, Stanford, Calif., 1947.

Roosevelt, Elliott, *FDR: His Personal Letters, 1928–1945,* 2 vols., Duell, Sloan and Pierce, New York, 1950.

Ross, Hugh, "Roosevelt's Third Term Nomination," *Mid-America,* 44 (1962).

Rudolph, Frederick, "The American Liberty League, 1934–1940," *American Historical Review,* 56 (1950).

Ruetten, Richard T., "Showdown in Montana, 1938: Burton Wheeler's Role in the Defeat of Jerry O'Connell," *Pacific Northwest Quarterly,* 54 (1963).

Salyers, James E., "The Politics of Depression: the Emergence and Eclipse of the Democratic Party in Missouri: A County-State Continuum, 1928-1944," *Missouri Historical Society Bulletin,* 25 (1968).

Sanford, Fillmore H., "Public Orientation to Roosevelt," *Public Opinion Quarterly,* 15 (1951).

Scammon, Richard M., *America at the Polls,* University of Pittsburgh Press, Pittsburgh, 1965.

Schaffer, Alan, *Vito Marcantonio, Radical in Congress,* Syracuse University Press, Syracuse, 1966.

Schmidtlein, Ronald, "Harry S Truman and the Pendergast Machine," *Midcontinent American Studies Journal,* 7 (1966).

Schwarz, Jordan A., *The Interregnum of Despair: Hoover, Congress and the Depression,* University of Illinois Press, Urbana, 1970.

Shanks, Alexander G., "Sam Rayburn and the New Deal, 1933-1936," unpublished doctoral dissertation, University of North Carolina, Chapel Hill, 1964.

———, "Sam Rayburn: the Texas Politician as a New Dealer," *East Texas Historical Journal,* 5 (1967).

Shenton, James P., "The Coughlin Movement and the New Deal," *Political Science Quarterly,* 73 (1958).

Shively, W. Phillips, "A Reinterpretation of the New Deal Realignment," *Public Opinion Quarterly,* 35 (1971).

Skates, John R., "From Enchantment to Disillusionment: a Southern Editor Views the New Deal," *Southern Quarterly,* 5 (1967).

———, "Journalist vs. Politician: Fred Sullens and Theodore G. Bilbo," *Southern Quarterly,* 8 (1970).

Stave, Bruce M., *The New Deal and the Last Hurrah: Pittsburgh Machine Politics,* University of Pittsburgh Press, Pittsburgh, 1970.

———, "The New Deal, the Last Hurrah and the Building of an Urban Political Machine," *Pennsylvania History,* 33 (1966).

Sternsher, Bernard, *Hitting Home: the Great Depression in Town and Country,* Quadrangle, Chicago, 1970.

Stoesen, Alexander R., "The Senatorial Career of Claude D. Pepper," unpublished doctoral dissertation, University of North Carolina, Chapel Hill, 1964.

Strickland, Arvarh, "The New Deal Comes to Illinois," *Illinois State Historical Society Journal,* 63 (1970).

Sundquist, James L., *Dynamics of the Party System: Alignment and Realignment of Political Parties in the United States,* Brookings Institution, Washington, D. C., 1973.

Sussman, Leila A., *Dear FDR: a Study of Political Letter-Writing,* Bedminster Press, Totowa, N. J., 1963.

———, "FDR and the White House Mail," *Public Opinion Quarterly,* 20 (1956).

Tobin, Sidney, "The Early New Deal in Baton Rouge as Viewed by the Daily Press," *Louisiana History,* 10 (1969).

United States Senate, 75th Congress, 1st Session, Report #151, *Investigation of Campaign Expenditures in 1936.* U. S. Government Printing Office, Washington, D. C., 1937.

Wecter, Dixon, *The Age of the Great Depression,* Macmillan, New York. 1948.

Weiss, Stuart L., "Maury Maverick and the Liberal Bloc," *Journal of American History,* 57 (1971).

146

Wickens, James F., "The New Deal in Colorado," *Pacific Historical Review,* 38 (1969).

Wolfskill, George, *Revolt of the Conservatives: a History of the American Liberty League, 1934-1940,* Houghton-Mifflin, Boston, 1962.

———, and John A. Hudson, *All But the People: Franklin D. Roosevelt and His Critics, 1933-1939,* Macmillan, New York, 1969.

Young Edwin, and Milton Derber, *Labor and the New Deal,* University of Wisconsin Press, Madison, 1957.

Zeigler, Luther H., Jr., "Sen. Walter George's 1938 Campaign," *Georgia Historical Quarterly,* 43 (1959).

Index